six men

encountering God

Text copyright © Brad Lincoln 2008
The author asserts the moral right
to be identified as the author of this work

Published by
The Bible Reading Fellowship
15 The Chambers, Vineyard
Abingdon, OX14 3FE, United Kingdom
Website: www.brf.org.uk

ISBN 978 1 84101 528 6
First published 2008
10 9 8 7 6 5 4 3 2 1 0

Acknowledgments
Unless otherwise stated, scripture quotations taken from the Holy Bible, New International
Version, copyright © 1973, 1978, 1984 by International Bible Society, are used by permission
of Hodder & Stoughton Publishers, a division of Hodder Headline Ltd. All rights reserved.
'NIV' is a registered trademark of International Bible Society. UK trademark number 1448790.

A catalogue record for this book is available from the British Library

Printed in Singapore by Craft Print International Ltd

six men

encountering God

Brad Lincoln

Acknowledgments

Morna, you believed and hoped in me and in God when I despaired. Without you, I would have never had the courage to start or the endurance to complete this project. Don't ever believe you are in a shadow: you pour forth light. I love you.

To M, A, P, S, S and J. It was a privilege just to hear your stories. Thank you for sharing them and for your bravery in releasing them.

To Jeffrey Archer and Philip Yancey. You both unwittingly helped me get this book off my chest. One of you made me realize that getting a book published is perhaps not that difficult, and therefore allowed me to think that I might have a chance. The other showed me just how high a standard I need to reach, if the book is to be worth reading.

The men whose stories appear in this book have been both honest and open. They have agreed that their identities do not need to be hidden and they stand by all that is written here. The events are recorded through their eyes. But most of the names that appear in this book are of those who brushed up against the main subjects, and it has been impossible to contact all these people to get their perspective on the events recounted. For that reason, and because none of us would wish to be the cause of offence, the names that appear in the book have been changed. I hope that has not removed the authenticity of the stories. Just like the tongue, the pen is a powerful weapon that must be used with as much care and craft as possible. If you recognize yourself in this book, if you feel mis-represented, then please forgive me. No injury is intended.

Contents

✣

Foreword

There is little doubt in my mind that the 1995 Rugby World Cup in South Africa is the reason I have been asked to write a foreword to this book—or any other book, for that matter.

South Africa played the All Blacks from New Zealand, one of the greatest teams in the world, for the ultimate crown—to become World Champions. We reached the final against all odds; we had one shot at the title, one opportunity to seize everything we had always wanted. The game was ferocious, fast, tough and unforgiving. When the referee blew the whistle on full time, the scores were level and we had to play 30 minutes of extra time.

The final five minutes were nerve-racking as my team edged ahead. When the referee blew the final whistle, I spontaneously sank to my knees and closed my eyes.

In a flash I was surrounded by my team mates. Not everyone was a Christian—some were Jewish and some did not believe at all—but as we huddled together, I asked one of our team mates, Chester Williams (who was a fellow Christian), to say 'thank you' to the Lord for being blessed to play in such an amazing game. With bedlam breaking out around the stadium and across our country, we quietly bowed our heads together in thanks and appreciation for the opportunity to live our dreams.

What captured the imagination of the sporting world was the picture of me raising the William Webb Ellis trophy above my head, eyes closed. Nelson Rolihlahla Mandela had been released from prison a mere three years before the World Cup and he stood next to me with his arms raised triumphantly. The smile on his face said it all.

Madiba, as he is affectionately known in South Africa, did not wear a suit for this special occasion. He wore the Springbok jumper which, to the majority of South Africans, was a symbol of apartheid, but on that day it became a symbol of pride and unity.

My eyes were closed because I was saying 'thank you' for the second time in 20 minutes. I was saying 'thank you' for being such a privileged individual, for being at the right place at the right time, for wisdom to make the right decisions. Thank you, Lord, for giving me the opportunity to play the sport I love.

Let me rewind: I grew up in apartheid South Africa. I went to an all-white Afrikaans school and never debated politics, for what you see is what you believe. At the age of six, while most of my friends went to church, I played with other boys in the park. I eventually became intrigued, though, and one Sunday morning I declared to my parents that I was going to church—on my own.

I wanted to learn more about the Lord and see for myself what this church business was all about. What I discovered was an amazing relationship, and it was because of that relationship that I closed my eyes in front of millions of people all over the world to say 'thank you' to the Lord.

This book tells the stories of six men who encountered the Lord for themselves in different ways and different places, and found that knowing him made all the difference. I hope that you will enjoy it and find inspiration here for your own journey.

I met Brad Lincoln through a mutual friend and have only admiration for what he has achieved. His faith and his commitment to others have been the driving force in his life. He has travelled all over the world, with the Lord walking next to him; many people's lives have been changed for the better as a result.

Francois Pienaar

·:·

Introduction

Ever-increasing circles

I have never understood how this world works. In fact, it was only recently that I realized I assume that it does work. For a brief while, I flirted with the idea that it doesn't, but that seemed far too desperately pointless.

I think everybody knows how some South American species of butterfly hovering somewhere in the Andes might flutter a little too energetically and risk the creation of a tidal wave off the coast of China. They call it chaos theory. But no matter how much of a mess this world seems and how random our lives feel, I have to believe that an unseen hand is involved. You see, even for those who sub-scribe to chaos theory, the butterfly is a potential planet killer only if it works in perfect harmony with an infinite number of other seemingly unconnected events—perhaps if a tree falls in an Austrian valley, a man drops his ice cream in Blackpool and, with perfect timing in a New York zoo, a monkey sneezes...

The chaos theorist and the atheist are both forced to believe that they are living in a terrifyingly random world, where the next time they turn the page of a book too quickly they could unwittingly cause David Beckham to change his hairstyle six months later. The Christian has to believe, however, that it is all a conspiracy.

This is the conundrum. The Bible teaches us that as individuals we all have free will to choose what we do next. However, it also tells us that God is in control of what happens in the world, even to the extent of creating and destroying empires: 'For the Scripture says to Pharaoh: "I raised you up for this very purpose, that I might display my power in you and that my name might be proclaimed in all the earth." Therefore God has mercy on whom he wants to have mercy, and he hardens whom he wants to harden' (Romans

9:17–18). I think we can assume that Pharaoh was ignorant of his appointment as God's accomplice. He would have believed he was making his own decisions, acting independently of his own volition. So if we are acting freely, independently, how can Mr Big be behind it all?

It was during the hot, humid monsoon in Nepal that my wife and I made a decision in response to a situation. We thought it was free will.

We had travelled to a Nepali village about three or four hours' walk uphill from the nearest road. Despite its relative isolation, Arthar is a sizeable community of over 5000 people, sprawling either side of a ridge some 5500 feet above sea level. We were part of a group of eight *bideshi* (foreigners) and two Nepali language teachers, staying for two weeks with some of the families in the village. The purpose was to help us in our language learning, understanding of the culture and appreciation of the living conditions of the majority of Nepalis. At that point, we had only been in Nepal for three months and we quickly became aware that, even with our numerous orientation lectures and experience of the relatively affluent city of Pokhara, there was much to learn. For a start, despite being led around the steep, rain-slicked, red mud paths of the village by surefooted villagers wearing plastic and foam flip-flops, we showed a Bambi-like inability to stay on our feet. The villagers were both gentle and understanding, resisting the temptation to laugh as I slid into yet another rice paddy.

We had been there five days when we first met Laxmi and her daughter Kalpana. We had not intended to return to the house in which we were staying, but a change of plan caused us to wander into the courtyard about midway through this particular Saturday afternoon. Initially the scene looked quite innocent. From her clothes, the absence of jewellery, even the texture of her skin, it was obvious that the woman washing the pots in the water supply of the house was poor. Her small daughter was sleeping beside her under a pile of rags in the warm afternoon sun. 'How nice,' we naïvely assumed. 'The woman of the house is clearly letting her neighbour use the tap to wash her pots and pans.'

It subsequently became apparent that the woman was actually washing our host's pots as a way to earn some food: two cobs of corn. It was taking her some time, mainly because she had cataracts in both eyes, rendering her almost completely blind. The 'pile of rags' her daughter was sleeping under were, in fact, the daughter's clothes. Morna, my wife, peeled away the urine-soaked material to discover a severely malnourished child, too weak to sit or stand. She had a high temperature, indicating a fever. Her swollen cheeks, feet and hands were symptoms of circulation problems, probably caused as her organs struggled in the absence of badly needed vitamins. Although the child was four years old, Morna was able to dress her in our nine-month-old son's shorts and T-shirt, so that her other 'clothes' could be washed. We were later able to estimate her weight at five kilos.

We quickly discovered from the other villagers that the woman was extremely poor, with no other family and nowhere to live. We went to the only shop in the village and bought five days' supply of rice and vegetables to enable the pair to feed themselves. Morna walked with them to where they were staying, carrying the child and the food. She returned in tears, and told me that their 'home' was a covered space between two buildings where rice sacks were stored, open to the elements. The tears were because it was apparent to Morna that, without urgent treatment, the girl was going to die.

We had to decide what to do. I am embarrassed to say that we actually considered, albeit briefly, that there might be nothing we could reasonably do. In the end, what made us act was the belief that, in our shoes, Jesus would never have turned his back on this woman. So we flapped our butterfly wings, feeling quite flimsy but hoping we could create some sort of wave. In the next couple of days, we consulted the village leader, bought some locally available medicines, evaluated the locally available health post and then cut short our stay in the village to take the woman and child to the nearest city, Pokhara. The sight of them being carried to the road by porters was enough to convince us we were on the right track.

There followed a hospital stay of eight days for Kalpana and her mother while the child received first intravenous treatment and then dietary supplements. It became apparent that at the root of her rapid decline was nothing more exceptional than a case of worms— a nuisance to most healthy kids but all too frequently life-threatening in Nepal. During this time it was possible, with the help of many of our new friends within our missionary organization, to arrange the operations required to restore Laxmi's eyesight and to begin the work of providing a basic home, some basic employment training and a school for Kalpana. Three weeks after we had gone to Pokhara, we were able to return the two of them to their village with a future—admittedly still a tough and difficult future but, with Laxmi's restored eyes, literally a brighter future.

We had done something—taken a decision and acted on it. We did it prayerfully, true, but *we* did it. I have come to think of this action like throwing a pebble into a pond, because the consequences of our intervention have been considerable. The ripples have spread. Some unexpected events have occurred and developments have taken place in unexpected directions. However, all of these other events have happened only because others have also decided to take some action. They too have thrown pebbles and, as the rings have expanded, their ripples have intersected with ours, creating new patterns.

Before we ever visited the village, another family had left a Bible with the shopkeeper from whom we bought the food for the woman and her child. He asked us where in the Bible it suggested that we should pray for people for healing, and we were able to show him. A Nepali Christian, one of our language teachers, had been seeking a way to witness to his boss, who had become disillusioned with some of the injustices of the caste system and his Hindu traditions. When we cut short our stay in the village to work with the woman, it caused the boss to go to the teacher and discuss the motives behind our action. A Christian Nepali social worker was aware of a woman in his church who was very short of money. We were able to employ her to feed and care for Laxmi and Kalpana in hospital, providing a source of income with dignity for a couple of weeks. While she was in the hospital, she witnessed to her patients. One Nepali church was discussing how the *bideshi* visitors who first brought the gospel didn't seem to care for Nepalis 'the way they used to', yet, among the reminiscences of the older church members, this more recent example of compassion for Laxmi and Kalpana was shared by one individual, and the church meeting was greatly encouraged and challenged.

Not all of the consequences were positive. Our action caused some controversy within our own organization, with some people questioning the wisdom of helping this woman in the way that we did. They suggested that our actions were naïve, that it was likely that all we had done was to postpone the inevitable. Some, with much more experience in Nepal than I, suggested that we were lucky and that we risked creating more problems than we had solved. Among other things, we appeared to have created a storm in a teacup.

So where was God in all this? As I sat outside one of the many tea shops, considering what was going on, I had ample opportunity to watch raindrops causing rings of ripples in puddles. The ripples in the muddy street puddles intersected and interacted and, as they did so, they created new patterns. In these interference patterns, some ripples joined with others to create bigger waves while others cancelled each other out. While one big splash on its own could sometimes affect the whole puddle, in combination with others it created new and unpredictable patterns.

It made me think that perhaps every action we take is like that of a waterboatman or other insect struggling on the surface of a pond.

Our writhing arms and bodies make little ripples, beyond our understanding. Our vibrations reach across the water, always spreading, and, as they spread, interacting and interfering with each other. Perhaps God sometimes reaches down to touch the surface and make grand ripples of his own, both affecting us directly and causing waves that swamp or multiply our own efforts—and somehow, God always manages to make the result look beautiful. From our vantage point, stuck to the tension on the surface, it looks choppy as we sink in a trough and waves obscure the horizon, while at other times we are lifted on a crest to get a better perspective. Yet from God's point of view, it never looks chaotic. It looks exactly the way he meant it to look.

That's a comforting theory, but how do we check it out? I reasoned that if God was working with and through Pharaoh at the time of Moses—if he was involved in everything—then he would have been involved in my life before I even acknowledged his existence. I began to think through my developing years, my own story, searching for his fingerprints. It didn't take me long to discover what I believe to be his signature on many of my preconversion experiences. I started to write them down and, in recording them, to search for patterns and clues to God's methods and techniques. In so doing, I hoped to learn more about him. In the same way that scientists try to understand the characteristics of subatomic particles too small to see, by studying the traces they leave as they race through baths of chlorine buried beneath mountains, so I was searching for God in the patterns his interference had left in my life.

This book has been an attempt to expand that process. I have had the great privilege of sitting and listening to a number of men telling their true stories, allowing me to spot patterns with them and draw conclusions from their experiences. I am immensely grateful to them just for that. I hope and believe that we have all learnt things from the hours spent chatting. The fact that these men have then agreed to allow me to write their stories down as best I can, and to share them, is beyond the call of duty. They have shown great honesty, openness and bravery of a type not normally associated with the male of the species.

I have chosen to write their stories in the first person, to emphasize the very personal nature of our interactions with God. I've had to try to put myself in the other man's shoes, to look through his eyes and interpret through his mind. The result can, of course, only be an approximation. While I have worked with the subjects closely in reproducing events that took place as long as 50 years ago, we view the events through the distorting lenses of memory, interpretation and assumption. Nonetheless, I believe that these stories of men who would describe themselves as 'ordinary' are quite remarkable and worthy of examination. I hope and pray that you can identify with these characters and, in doing so, can draw your own patterns and conclusions about the nature of our God. You may feel you know him well or you may doubt he exists at all, but these stories have convinced me more than ever before that he knows you. In fact, he is getting involved, interfering with you, even now.

Ask yourself this: why did you open this book?

✣

Peak experience

The great lesson... that the sacred is in the ordinary, that it is to be found in one's daily life, in one's neighbours, friends, and family, in one's back yard, and that travel [pilgrimages] may be a flight from confronting the sacred—this lesson can be easily lost. To be looking elsewhere for miracles is to me a sure sign of ignorance that everything is miraculous.

Abraham Maslow, 'Religions, Values and Peak Experiences' (Penguin, 1976)

Basically, I could not hold on much longer. All of the options were exhausted and so was I. My arms had that slightly heavy, dying feeling that comes as the muscles, having topped themselves up with lactic acid, are running out of sugar to burn. In contrast with the likely violence of my end, they were giving up slowly—gradually, but surely. Not that my tiredness made much difference. This would have been an impossible position if it had come at the beginning of the climb, with my body still warm and elastic, blood surging through my limbs just for the sheer excitement of being alive. As it was, the Norwegian winter sun had already gone and, with it, any last vestiges of warmth and hope. In the grey-blue light I could feel the cold coming at me like an approaching freight train, not rushing like an express but slow and inevitable. It would not smash into me; it would slowly squeeze the life out of me bit by bit. I could see it coming, could do nothing about it, did not care. I fully expected to die of the fall long before the cold got me. It was just, somehow, an appropriate atmosphere for an unspectacular failure.

It was not a good day to die. I would not be going out in a blaze of glory. It might be worth two column inches on page 22 of the *Daily Telegraph*, but it would be written off as an inevitable consequence of stupid decisions and ill-equipped climbers taking one risk too many. I would receive a glowing obituary at college and (ironically enough) my fellow climbers would turn out at the funeral my parents would organize in the Lincolnshire chapel I never frequented.

They say that on big climbs at high altitude there are mornings when everyone feels they are at the beginning of a day that will end in tragedy, but the really successful climbers are the ones who know when the feeling is a true reflection of the circumstances. The really good climbers know when to turn back.

I could have turned back. Arne did. Even as the least experienced of the three of us, he had realized that our progress was too slow and we were not going to make the summit of the Ottafössen waterfall before dark. So, showing strength of character, resisting the 'up, up, up' urge of the climber's inner voice, he had abseiled off the vertical ribbon of ice. Steve and I had said a rapid farewell, then Arne had headed back to the station waiting-room at the isolated railway junction where we had persuaded the staff to let us sleep the night before, in cheerful warmth. While he descended, we had pushed on up the brittle ice. It was not how winter climbing should be. Our ascent had thus far been characterized by an unsatisfactory scrambling to find decent placements for our axes—smashing and fracturing the frozen surface of the waterfall. When we did find purchase, there was no real confidence but rather a nervy half-trust in the hold, and hesitant progress, limbs and senses taut for the moment when the tip of the angled ice-axe blade would rip out.

About 40 or 50 feet from the top of the vertical mile of rock and ice, Steve and I had found relative safety in a small ice cave. When it became time to move on again, he had taken up a stance secured to a couple of fragile icicles, more in hope that he would never have to rely on them than in the expectation that they would be any use in the case of a big fall. Emerging from the cave, I tiptoed a traverse of 30 or 40 feet, the front points of my crampons finding enough purchase to allow me to make the horizontal journey across a glassy smooth wall. I had headed for the one apparent weakness in the route, a vertical crack full of loose fragments of ice, and wedged

16

myself into it. In that relative security, I had placed our two remaining ice screws as high as I could manage and had clipped the line into them. These would be my first line of defence if I did fall, and I had absolutely no confidence in them, given the quality of the ice we had thus far encountered.

In climbing, there are distinct moments of commitment, and this was one. I could have turned back at this point, but instead I shouted to Steve that I was going to have a go, and started to scramble my way up the crack. This was no elegant series of coordinated and planned moves, but an undignified thrashing of feet and ice-axes—more often than not, achieving a cascade of ice rather than any upward progress. It was all pretty ungainly. Eventually, breathing heavily and with the cold stinging my nostrils, I came to the point at which the crack diminished to nothing and, with it, the option to continue straight up.

I half twisted and half shoved myself round and managed to get myself in a precarious position from which I could see out to the right, and found no reassurance. Away and up, there swept a barely rippled wall of blue-white frosted glass, beautiful in its lack of imperfections to anyone less directly involved. To me it spelt the end. My left foot was trembling slightly as my calves spent themselves with the effort of holding steady in the crack, and my left hand was repeatedly hacking and scrabbling to find a placement for the teeth of the axe in the same groove. My body was curved around the right-hand edge of the crack, with my right hand and foot slapping and flapping helplessly at the flat ice surface.

I could not see how I could get out on to the wall to try to climb it and, even if I could, I was certain I did not have the energy, ability or equipment to make any meaningful progress. It was also clear that I would not have the strength to maintain my 'half-in, half-out' position for more than a few minutes. I tried to fight the burgeoning fear that was reaching up from my stomach and squeezing at my lungs, allowing me ever shorter and shallower breaths. The blood, desperately trying to respond to the many demands for oxygen from my muscles, thumped in my neck, ears and temples. I tried to focus on the options. There were none. I could not climb on; I could not stay here; I would never be able to retrace my route down the crack. I was going to fall.

Steve, 50 or 60 feet below me and attached to me by the nylon rope, was not as acutely aware of his own personal danger. When I fell, I would drop past him and, having accelerated for over 100 feet, I would take up any remaining slack in the rope and simply drag him out of the cave and down the frozen watercourse with me. We would both fall at least 2000 feet. If, by some small miracle, either of us survived the impact, he would die where he lay, injured at the bottom, with no one looking for us, miles from the next human being, alone and tied to a frozen corpse. I worked through the logic of the situation and then gave up on logic. My sum total of resources had proved insufficient. Nothing I had learnt, no equipment I had brought with me, no technique or training or temperament, would be enough. I gave in to fear and prayed.

I guess I could have prayed to the ice, to the sky, to the disappearing sunlight or even to the moon that must have been rising somewhere. People have done that before, and at least I had tangible evidence of their existence. Perhaps it was my mother's faith, which, though unspoken, was definitely there throughout my childhood, or maybe it was the few weeks I attended that chapel Sunday school as a kid. Whatever the reason, I prayed a not terribly unique or original prayer to God. I attempted to strike the bargain that almost everyone has used as a refuge of panicked last resort, whether for a genuine life-and-death situation or just to see their team escape relegation at the end of the season: 'Get me out of this, God. Just get me out of this and I'll do anything you want. Anything.'

How many people have struck that deal, never once considering their own obligations if God does indeed grant the wish? I had more than enough to occupy my mind without considering a future series of commitments and, with no obvious alternatives, it was a bargain offered like a bankrupt's wedding ring in return for a lottery ticket.

My future—the only thing of value left, and that was rapidly depreciating—offered in return for my future existence. It was an easy deal to make: zero additional risk and, no matter how poor the odds, a potential jackpot return.

'Trust me.'

I can't say with conviction that God actually spoke to me. Not in words. It was more a vague but powerful sense that God was there and that he wanted me to trust him. If the presence of God can be likened to any elemental force, then I guess I had an experience not unlike that of the prophet Elijah when he too emerged from a fault in the rock. There was a whispering from some amorphous cloud around me and inside me, rather than the caricatured thundering voice from on high. Ephemeral as this sense now sounds, at the time it was substantial enough for me to lean on, almost literally.

I pulled back my heavy right arm and swung it half blind at the ice above and to the right of my head. 'Let this be a good one,' I whispered inwardly, trying to engage the Unknown in conversation. The blow was genuinely made in pure baseless hope, and so I registered the dull 'thok' with some surprise as the tip of the axe found a good solid placement. It is pretty rare to find such a hold first time and especially when swung blind. I dragged my left arm out from the crack and swung again. 'Thok.' Two good placements. I can't tell you what my reaction was to the second miracle, because at this point I stopped thinking. I just climbed.

I want to emphasize the word 'just' in that last little phrase. How often in your life have you ever done 'just' one thing? How many times have you ever been so absorbed and concentrated that nothing else—not one single distracting thought—entered your consciousness? I didn't consider the new sense of trust, I didn't notice the ache in my forearms, I was oblivious to the cold, and I was even oblivious to the fact that I was oblivious. I just climbed. One after another, perfect ice-axe placements flowed together with flawless positioning of the front points on my crampons. In my altered state of perception, I saw tiny fluctuations in the colour of the ice and understood their meaning as they showed me the lines of weakness. I moved automatically, in harmony with my body, the equipment and even the ice itself. And then I was at the top.

It was probably, in total, a vertical distance of 30 feet, and it can only have taken ten minutes. I sat quite still, shocked by what had just happened, waiting for the sensation to pass. In my heightened state, the full-ish moon provided plenty of light, illuminating my breath as it curled upwards in the cold. The sweet dry smell of the pine trees that crowded up towards the edge of the precipice was aromatherapy. Moments passed as my rate of breathing and my surging pulse subsided and I again became a normal human, left with only a wide-eyed memory of my supernatural escape. I remembered Steve and, quickly tying the rope to the secure and solid trunks of the pines as a belay, I half assisted, half dragged him up from the cave below.

As he crawled over the lip, he spoke his own disbelief. 'How the —— did you get up that?' I can't remember the exact words, but I am pretty sure he would have used some expletive I'm glad I cannot repeat. I knew the answer. I'd just had a Peak Experience.

I'd been reading a lot about this elusive holy grail—the Peak Experience. My recent life had been very deliberately structured around climbing. The availability of subsistence grants, the long holidays, the proximity of like-minded friends, not to mention the presence of climbing guru Pete Livesey as a lecturer, had made it easy to select the academic backwater of Ilkley College as the best place to spend four years scraping through a B.Ed. in Outdoor Education. For my dissertation, I had chosen to write about a phenomenon that peppered the pages of various climbing magazines: Abraham Maslow's 'Peak Experience'. Primarily looking at states described by religious mystics, he articulated moments where the individual becomes 'most truly himself, more perfectly actualizes his potentials, closer to the core of his Being, more fully human'. Although he initially interviewed a variety of gurus, prophets and those active in the creative arts, it was Maslow's assertion that the housewife and the athlete are equally capable of participating in these spiritual moments of self-actualization (to use the jargon) that allowed the rest of us to climb on board. He famously wrote that in the attempt to reach the heights, 'a first rate soup is better than a second rate painting', and many mountaineers would add 'summiting a great climb' to the list.

I especially recall reading John Long's description of weaving in and out of the rock as he ascended a big wall without the security of a safety rope, in characteristically romantic language. In tennis they were beginning to call it 'Inner Tennis.' Later came Inner Skiing and then Inner everything else. Californian climbers were using their own wacky phrase for it: 'think pink'. As far as I was concerned, it sounded like the effects of smoking a little too much weed, combined with an adrenalin surge, producing a particular relaxed focus that could be described in terms of biochemistry and basic psychology—that and the desire to talk like a hippy.

My development through childhood and adolescence had given me a fairly solid Protestant work ethic, from which spirituality had been thoroughly excised and in which brief moments of achievement were earnt through long hours of effort and personal investment. I preferred fairly rounded and very grounded companions to those who had cruised through life riding the up-escalator of privilege. Stairs were there to be climbed, and the top floor should be gained with a knowledge that one had earnt the right to be there. There is no magic. You get out what you put in.

My mother, a regular at her local Lincolnshire chapel, provided an example of 'religious' life. Chapel-going was about religious and regular attendance, which placed faith in a compartment found only in the pews. I had never seen her open a Bible or pray outside the stone walls. She had never spoken to me openly about Christianity and, although I was taken to Sunday school during my early years, I was given the choice of attending as soon as I was able to make it. By the age of twelve I had exercised the option to abstain.

Looking back, it seems that my father had a more definite influence on my world view. His dreams were for dreaming, his life was for working, and these two spheres were strictly compart-mentalized. His values were based on investment and self-sacrifice for the family, ancestry rooted in the Lincolnshire soil. The family were (indeed, some still are) small-scale 'cottager' farmers, although my father's father was a docks policeman on the east coast. Starting as a butcher's errand runner, moving through postal delivery and National Service, Dad achieved the heady heights of white collar employment with the Department of Health and Social Security. His was a life lived in very civil service both to country and kin, enduring a despised job, dispensing public benefits to achieve a fiscal and status benefit for his loved ones. While I subconsciously soaked up many of his values, I positively grabbed at his aspirations.

The anecdotes that brought Dad's passions to the surface were those that described his youthful cycle touring expeditions. His favourite books were as practical and pragmatic as his lifestyle, but they described the best way to build a fire, tie a knot, whittle a tent peg or construct a bivouac. I absorbed the contents from early on, and lived out the dreams under tents made from towels and clothes horses. Youth and its associated freedom from responsibility allowed me to indulge my dreams in a way that Dad could not. We were both bored by our nine-to-fives, but for me the tedious school day was an interlude between evenings and weekends focused on the outdoor life. Like most children, I was forthright about the things I wanted, pushing and pestering my parents. The start of a Cub Scouts pack in a neighbouring village gave me an opportunity to feed this hunger and, at the age of nine, I joined. Even amid the exuberance of the pack, I was by far the most enthusiastic. As a consequence, I achieved the promotions and badges that the Scout Association confers on its rank and file, but they were merely a byproduct of my interest in all things outdoor and adventurous.

Football supporters live their lives in seasons and Saturdays, while Scouts measure the passing of time in summer camps and evening meetings. Coincident with my elevation from the Cubs to the Scouts was the move to a secondary school. It is therefore ironic that while the opportunities afforded by the Scout troop were eagerly antici- pated, it was an event in the first year of secondary school that brought a clearer focus to my passions and ultimately pulled me away from Scouting. Our class was taken on a week-long trip to Barmouth on the Welsh coast, at which we were given taster sessions in orienteering, canoeing and, crucially, rock climbing. It was my first experience of climbing and its associated sensuous paraphernalia— slings, karabiners, harnesses and ropes. I was hooked.

The following Easter, I joined a group from the Scouts on a hiking trip in the Peak District, during which we pitched our camp for a night under a crag called Birchens Edge. Even now I can clearly recall the morning. I woke early. For many, the response to the cold, damp tent walls was to shrink back into the warmth of the sleeping bag. I distinctly remember hearing, beyond the canvas, the voices of people at the foot of the crag. They beckoned me and a few of the others out of our cocoons and across the dewy grass to watch 'proper' climbers in action. A gulf opened up that I ached to cross. We were boys playing at the outdoors, learning as we went. The men coiling ropes, chatting casually about routes, smoking their cigarettes and pushing themselves past fingertip holds, dotting the rock with chalk marks, were living my dreams. For the first time I understood what graduation meant, and I wanted to study. School was to be endured, climbing was worthy of my personal commit- ment, and, with an objective forming somewhere in my gut, it became clear just how much of my dad's capacity to invest I had inherited.

The next weekend, I persuaded a friend to join me and we hitched our way from home back to Birchens Edge. Once there, we clambered our amateur way around the base of the rock, copying our new heroes, in our minds emulating them, before making the two-hour return trip.

My Scout troop was both active and adventurous, and I was a fully paid-up member. The dues were not financial but physical, allowing those who contributed effort and ideas free rein. One weekend, we held a sponsored canoe race in which my team prevailed and therefore earned a key say in the use of the money raised. While others struggled to come up with a coherent plan, I was in no such quandary. We should buy some climbing equipment. Our leader, Dick, agreed, adopting the plan with characteristic verve. These were days when adventure was unfettered by cautious consideration of legalities. Litigious parents were only found in the caricatures of the upper classes in comics and novels, so the fact that Dick had as much experience of climbing as he had of writing liability disclaimers was not a brake on our enthusiasm. As far as I was concerned, he had all the key qualifications—energy, a willingness to support us in our own passions, and a Sherpa.

The Sherpa was an orange builders' van, and four or five hardcore enthusiasts from our troop spent every other weekend bouncing in the back on top of sleeping bags, rags and old foam mats laid down to ease the hard cold of the steel floor. Dick took the wheel as we headed for Wales or the Peak District or the Yorkshire Dales in search of rock faces and caves. Once there, we would drag out the kit we had assembled and work out for ourselves the right way to rig a belay, place the protecting nuts or master a layback. I took the lead role in the desk research, ordering books from the library in Lincoln, matching the line diagrams on the pages to our experiences, discovering new techniques to practise at the rock face on the following Saturday.

I continued to make repeated trips to Birchens Edge on the days when the Sherpa was not called into action, most frequently hitchhiking with a friend. One of these occasions marked a development in my understanding of how far my own endeavours could take me. We had been watching a pair attempt a route. The first and more capable man led, taking the rope up and using a variety of aluminium devices to provide some protection should he fall. This is the more exposed role in climbing, where the safety of the climber depends almost entirely on the climber himself. His partner, holding the rope, can only save the climber from a fall if his friend above can safely place runners for the rope to travel through in the cracks. Much is said about the special relationship between the two members of a climbing team. The bond of the rope, where two are literally bound to each other, is as much about shared risk and mutual dependence as it is about the physical link. On relatively short climbs, however, where the top can be gained within one rope length, it is very much the leader who experiences the greater hazard and takes the responsibility.

As we watched, the first climber made it to the top. In the normal manner, having regained his breath, he set about finding a safe point from which to belay. He did this by finding a solid anchor point, such as a large boulder, round which he secured the rope, literally attaching himself to that foundation. He then passed the rope round and across his back before dropping it down to the second climber below. By shuffling the rope through his hands, he could take up any slack in the rope as the partner ascended, but hold it firm should the other fall.

On this occasion, and unfortunately for the second climber, he had an audience as he struggled to follow up the route, repeatedly slipping, trusting to the rope several times. Eventually, tired and dispirited, he admitted defeat and allowed himself to be lowered to the ground. To his credit, having failed himself, he turned to me and asked if I would like a go. It may be that his motive was actually to make it clear that this game is not as easy as it looks, and shared defeat is often easier to bear. Whatever, I was just grateful to have the chance. Unexpectedly I was clipped into a rope attached to a genuine climber—not exactly the big time, but certainly closer to bridging the gap than the clambering around a few feet from the ground that I had anticipated. I don't suppose it was in any way elegant, but to my great delight I worked my way to the top. I began to realize that the gulf could be bridged, that my ambitions could be realized. Hitherto, my sporting experience had not been one of success, and my failure to excel at school ball games had marked me out as one of the 'not sporty' types. These experiences are formative, and it may be that I was able to resist the defining nature of that particular epithet through small achievements like this success in climbing.

I have a deep sense of gratitude that, having found a passion, I could pursue it, and, as I watch the development of my own children, one of my recurring prayers is that they too will discover something in which they can find an enduring enthusiasm. The alternative, a life of indifference, is a lesser life.

Ironically, another factor that may have encouraged me in my quest to become a climber was that I lived in one of Britain's flattest counties. Despite the lack of millstone grit crags or even moderate hills, Lincolnshire's county town did boast a climbing club. I started to attend, cycling 14 miles into Lincoln to drink orange juice at the bar and soak up the atmosphere. The clubs based in the climbing hotbeds around the Peak and Lake Districts, and in North Wales, were populated by the 'names' of British climbing who regularly appeared in the magazines I read avidly. Climbing, like almost every other occupation, has its hierarchy. I would not regard myself as an especially talented young apprentice and I doubt I would have felt able to approach the stars who ascended the highest peaks and assumed corresponding status. To my good fortune, the top of the Lincolnshire tree was occupied by club members John Oaks and Geoff Causey. Neither had set the climbing world alight with any first ascents, but they had climbed routes that I had heard of. It was enough for now to be able to perch on a bar stool, sip my juice and listen to tales of daring, eavesdrop planning sessions, and breathe in the smoky exhalations of those who had been and done.

The lifestyle, the attitudes, the laconic conversation and the studied indifference infused my own development. I was invited first on day trips, then weekends, then minor expeditions. I grew and trained and developed, and, perhaps most importantly, *earned* my place. With the growth of technique and strength and ability came a deeper enhancement of my values. I well remember, some time later, looking slightly cynically at some colleagues as we travelled to climb one peak. They talked too much, wore their enthusiasm a little too openly and appeared to have come from privileged backgrounds where the accumulation of funds and equipment for their trips had not involved the sacrifice that respect required. My admiration was mainly reserved for those who had demonstrated dedication and denial, to live lives pursuing the summits.

The idea then that the climber can experience a super-spiritual moment was as foreign to me as the Nepali Sherpas who supported the Himalayan expeditions I aspired to join. The world in which I was involved valued very down-to-earth behaviour, and generally viewed the writings of the climbing mystics with a wry and mocking humour. To express an interest in these views was to invite a quick and sarcastic quip. Even exuberance in a climbing success had to be tempered with understatement, so it was both reasonable and safe for me to develop a scientific view about the 'Peak Experience'. I'd had good days, when I had climbed well or when I'd felt really on form. These moments could be attributed to hours of training in the gym or on the climbing wall, to special weather conditions, or to adrenalin surges followed by climactic moves, all played out against a background of beautiful scenery.

In the world of outdoor education (the subject of my B.Ed.), interest in providing people with the opportunity to experience such highs had been born out of Maslow's belief that problems such as alcoholism, violence and drug abuse stem from a spiritual emptiness that may be assuaged by even one 'Peak Experience'. Following his agenda, a number of 'outward bound' style courses emerged, in which adventure was offered to those who had never previously left an urban landscape. In the debate, I tended to disregard this approach as 'tinned adventure'—manufactured and artificial. In my research for my dissertation, I sought out articles providing chemical and physiological explanations. So it was my experience on that final pitch at the top of the frozen waterfall that forced me to allow for other possibilities. As I read articles on drug abuse, surfing and, of course, climbing, I began to discover that it was the more New Age writers, open to the inexplicable, who best described my own encounter.

That astonishing experience challenged my convictions about investment and return. The fact that I had had a Peak Experience was undeniable, but that I had earnt it was at best debatable. One could argue that I deserved to fall. I had ignored the warnings to turn back. I'd gone ill-equipped: I note, with a slight reddening of the cheeks, that I had not even been wearing a head torch as my twilight drama played out. I had committed the cardinal sin of climbing away from all of my options to leave myself stranded, with no route of advance or retreat. While Steve would not have deserved to be dragged off the mountain, I could not have blamed a fall on anyone other than myself. The idea that God may have answered my prayer was not justified by anything I had done in the immediately preceding moments or, indeed, at any point in my life.

The deal I struck with him was not based on any special faith, and up to that point I had offered him my indifferent tolerance, at best. He was, after all, confined to church services. So I am afraid that my return from Norway was not accompanied by any serious attempt to discover exactly what God might demand from me. He had kept his side of the deal, but I was not dwelling unduly on mine. The event may have allowed me to consider a role for the spiritual dimension within the physical, but I was preoccupied with an entirely different encounter. I had fallen in love with a fellow student, Amanda.

Of course, some of the attraction was physical. She was small, dark and athletic. I'd felt confident enough that she liked me to ask her out—but although she was quite shy, she'd had sufficient assurance to turn me down, and had kept me at a distance subsequently. In my attempt to handle this rejection and also to express my disbelief at her decision, I had written her a note. I returned to college with serious misgivings about the wisdom of my correspondence. When we did meet, she was good enough to address the key issue quickly, avoiding any prolonged tension: 'I'm sorry. I like you, but I am a Christian and you are not. It is too important a difference to ignore, so there can be no real relationship.'

This was a surprise. It was not the fact that she described herself as a Christian: I had known that she was a regular churchgoer. It was the idea that a faith could actually affect the way you lived that really gave me pause. It seemed pretty clear to me that she wanted a relationship, so she seemed to be concluding that her passion for Christ was of a higher priority than her interest in me. There he was again, if vicariously in this case. Twice in quick succession he had reached out from the confines of his own house to manipulate affairs in mine—once to save, once to deny. Or had he? Could I not rationalize it as some kind of yin-yang principle—a New Age, 'whole earth' concept of balance? He, She or It gives and takes away. The Force had been with me at least a couple of times, no doubt. It took me some time to discover an associated personality.

It is perhaps poetic that the eventual introduction was arranged by someone I could trace all the way back to that wall in Norway. Helen was another student on my college course. In the summer of 1984 she had a boyfriend, Brian. He was my climbing partner when I first went to the Troll Wall to see water cascading down its face, offering the dream of a winter ascent of a frozen waterfall. However, it was a full year after my icy epic and the warmer rejection by Amanda that I found myself in deep conversation with Helen. I had known for some time that Helen was also a committed Christian. She was someone I would never have described as 'religious', and she certainly shied away from the establishment and tradition, preferring a less conventional expression of her faith. Like any 'normal' student and climber, she was rebellious and passionate about many things. She did not fit into any caricature that I had developed based around the squarer Christian Union faithful: she preferred to be a more rounded peg.

I enjoyed the conversation, the walk home together from the pub, and the doorstep embrace that preceded our 'good night'. We became an item, Brian having long since departed the scene. Some two or three weeks later, we decided to travel down to Cornwall with a group of friends to spend some of the generous Easter holiday climbing. I would not be able to stay for the full break, as I had agreed to work as a cook for one week at the Buckden House Outdoor Centre in Wharfedale, West Yorkshire. The attraction of the job was that, having tidied up after breakfast, I would have most of the day free to work out on the climbing wall before getting dinner ready. The cash was already earmarked for an anticipated summer in the Alps. As an added bonus, my early departure from the team in Cornwall would allow me a day or so with Helen at her family's house in Devon on the way back up north.

It was in Cornwall that I had another of those pub conversations with Helen. In this case, it was pretty much one-way traffic, with her doing the talking. It was not that I was spellbound by her appearance, although she was undeniably attractive, with long, sun-bleached blonde hair framing a fresh face. It was not that she was especially forceful, and she certainly wasn't trying to dominate the tête-à-tête. I just found that I had nothing of significance to contribute. She, on the other hand, shared a series of life experiences that revealed a depth and substance I had never considered possible. She had grown up with her missionary parents in Thailand, and was able to recount childhood stories in which she encountered poverty and sickness, stories that were richer for the zest of an Asian culture and a family life lived with abundance and intensity. She had actually grown up in a mud hut and, on her return to the UK, had had to learn to hold a pen properly. While she sometimes appeared naïve, especially when displaying her ignorance of pop culture, hers was a life that operated on many levels, tapping into an underground spiritual reservoir and irrigating the surface to provide verdant fruit in varied colours and hues. As she continued talking in the pub, I began to feel rootless and monochrome. What you saw was all there was. My life seemed like a veneer, a façade, a superficial scrub anchored only in parched sand.

We walked back to the campsite almost mute. I had nothing to say. It was as if I was now enduring the very opposite of a Peak Experience—a Trough Experience. On that frozen waterfall I had received a glimpse of what was possible, a state that transcended normal humanness as I knew it, a moment when my body seemed inadequate to contain all that was possible. In a sense, I overflowed. Trudging along the clifftop path towards the tents, I now felt less than human. In comparison to Helen's apparent fullness, I felt like a hollow shell. I became aware that it was possible to look within a person, and when I looked within myself I found nothing.

A couple of days later, we broke the journey back north with the promised stay at Helen's parents' house. Over breakfast, Helen's father cornered me. He was, quite naturally, interested to find out exactly who his daughter was spending her time with, and where it was likely to be leading.

'What do you make of Jesus?'

It could have been a qualifying question, a selection interview test—one which, correctly answered, would have granted me access to his blessing, whatever that was. But now, as I look back, I detect his concern for me as much as for his daughter.

'I don't know. But I am genuinely interested to find out.'

I really, genuinely was. It occurs to me now that it would have been a great answer even if it had not been true, but I was still reeling from the discovery of my personal inner vacuum. Helen's dad gave me a paperback copy of the New Testament and suggested that this would be a good place to start. He also talked me through the sort of prayer I might use if I felt that I wanted to become more intimately involved with Jesus. He finished by assuring me that he would be praying for me. I'm not sure if I passed the 'suitable son-in-law' test, but the combination of Helen's substance and her father's frank certainty left me determined to discover more—genuinely determined, more determined than I had been as a result of that miraculous rescue and the deal I had struck in desperation.

You would have to understand just how addicted to climbing I was to realize how absurd it was for me to spurn the climbing wall to spend my free time reading the Bible. I loved climbing. It was not a hobby or an occupation or even a vocation. It had pretty much defined me. My time was divided between climbing, talking about climbing, and working out how I could do more climbing. I trained physically for it; I planned my life around it; I even once seriously considered credit card fraud to fund it. What I did not do was pass up an opportunity to spend time on a climbing wall to read about some bloke who had wandered around in the Middle East a couple of thousand years previously. Sure, he did ascend the odd mountain, but not on routes that would feature in anything more challenging than a pamphlet describing rambles in and around Jerusalem.

But, having arrived for the planned holiday job in Yorkshire, I did read avidly, for a good portion of each day. I made it all the way through Luke and even dipped occasionally into the more enigmatic Revelation. As I did so, Jesus rose up out of the pages as a real personality. He was not merely an interesting historical character but a flesh-and-blood, sitting-next-to-me, charismatic personality. He was alive, and I found that the more I read, the more I wanted to know. I read about the disciples who lived with this man and I realized that I was almost jealous. I wanted to be a disciple. I wanted to know him, really know him, genuinely know him. The moment at the top of the waterfall, Amanda's rejection, even the conversations with Helen can be seen as crucial moments only with the advantage of hindsight. In contrast, as I read that paperback New Testament I became aware that I was approaching a junction at which I would have to make a choice. I decided to go for a walk, a walk with a purpose. I would confront the issue. I decided to decide.

I did not head for the hills, but instead for the neighbouring village of Hubberholme, trudging a couple of miles through flurries of early afternoon snow falling from a frowning grey sky. I considered the options. I had believed that I had constructed my life on a fairly rational basis. A life spent climbing, scaling special peaks, seemed the best the planet had to offer. The conventional and rational alternatives of a life spent denying dreams, getting a normal job and becoming part of the establishment seemed particularly unattractive. On offer was a relationship with Christ and an acceptance of the divine as a source of inspiration and instruction. It offered an escape from the emptiness I had recently acknowledged —a chance of a deeper, more substantial life.

The small village church with its square stone tower was open and empty, with the midweek silence that only proper old churches can produce. Although it now has the claim of being the resting place for J.B. Priestley's ashes, in those days it was short of even that celebrity, and the oak pews, with their handcarved mice, were not enough to attract what little passing tourist trade the cold Yorkshire Dales can pull in at Easter. I took a hard seat a few rows back, allowing the atmosphere of cool reverence to add weight to my feelings. It seemed an appropriate location. He had come to my 'house' 15 months previously to leave his calling card, and it was only polite to return the compliment.

I prayed. 'I'm sorry that I have ignored you, God. I want to be a disciple. I want to leave my nets. I want to follow you.'

It was a nothing-to-lose swing of the ice-axe. If it didn't hold, I had lost nothing of significance, but if it did... To be honest, I am not sure I knew what to expect if it did hold. I wanted to get higher and this seemed to be the only chance. I swung the axe, not exactly sure what a firm placement would feel like.

'Thok.'

As I walked back, the snow heavier, it occurred to me that I had just become a Christian. I did not feel especially different. 'What happens next? What do I do now?' I wondered. I prayed again, 'You need to show me what direction to take.'

'Do what you will, do it well, and do it in my name.'

Again, not the thundering voice, even though the sky seemed to be in the mood for it. No distinctive spoken word, but a general sense of his affirmation of my decision. It was strangely comforting, allowing me to carry on with what I was doing but to shift the emphasis. Do it not for me, but for him. I certainly would not have understood at the time, but I now realize that my side of the bargain was being explained to me. I did not have to give up my ropes, leave my nets and wander off in some unspecified direction. He did not demand a denial of all that I enjoyed or knew. I was being asked to take on a new purpose. It ain't what you do, it's the *why* that you do it—and it gets results. The hole within me had been filled and I felt that I had become a man of substance. What was especially surprising was that I really did not deserve it. I had not earned the Peak Experience and, if anything, my tardiness in even considering my response to the waterfall miracle made me at best ungrateful, at worst a defaulter. Part of what fills me now is the joy and gratitude that he did not give up on me even then.

The Protestant work ethic handed down through family genera-tions is so pervasive that, although it has its origins in Christianity, it can actually mask the truth of a reward that is given freely. We certainly don't get what we deserve. I knew this already. From my thoughtful trudge back to cook dinner at Buckden House, I only had to glance back a couple of years to my early days at Ilkley College, to the time when the news of Dick's death was phoned through to me by my shocked parents.

You may remember Dick, owner of the orange Sherpa van. He had invested in me, and not only in me. He had enthused and infused many young boys, taking their aspirations and ideas and making them a reality. Never one to dismiss a mad scheme, he had shared his 'can do' attitude and, as a consequence, scattered over the world are some Lincolnshire lads who 'can do'. It was therefore cruel and undeserved that a lorry should shed its load and crush Dick's eight-year-old son, Michael. How can it be fair that one who moulded so many young lives was robbed of the chance to see the results of his efforts with his own son? How much crueller that he was even robbed of the enjoyment of seeing his surrogates develop, because shortly after this he too lost his life. Dick was caving with a friend of mine. Contradicting the weather forecast, a sudden downpour rapidly filled the cavern with water and, trapped underground, he drowned. Not only was he a big character, he was a big man, and it was his bulk that did not allow him to squeeze from the cave in time. My other, thinner friend escaped.

I recall being deeply shaken by the news. Young climbers feel a great certainty—a sense that while falls may happen, while there may be setbacks, they themselves are immune from disaster. My confidence was constructed upon a firm grounding in the work ethic that assures subscribers that the sweat of their own brow will at some point have its reward. Before Helen, before Amanda, before the Troll Wall in Norway, the first cracks in my scientific certainty may have been due to the injustice and shock of Dick's untimely end. I hope so. I hope that his death had a positive purpose and I hope that, somehow, he knows it.

Many times since then, I have been asked to tell the story of my commitment—my testimony. I've heard many others, including Elizabeth my wife, describe a time of consciously searching, like the merchant who trawls through the market stalls and backstreet bazaars in search of that one perfect pearl. I often choose to refer to another of the stories Jesus used to illustrate the experience of finding God. In one short verse in the Gospel of Luke, Jesus explains the kingdom of heaven in terms of a man who happens across a treasure hidden in a field. Having uncovered the trove, he hides it quickly, rushes off to sell everything he has and uses his new liquidity to buy the field, thus acquiring the right to the reward. It is in this way that I reconcile the competing philosophies and in them find peace.

Maslow was right. There is miraculous in the mundane, but there are also glimpses of the sublime in the misery and in the majestic. God can be found when we seek him, but reveals himself when we are focused on anything but him. There is mystery and there is collaboration and, just as God reveals himself in the most unlikely of circumstances, he also requires a willingness to make a personal investment. I can testify that my personal small investment has recouped. I've been overwhelmed, almost embarrassed by the reward.

If the hub cap fits

'Twas grace that taught my heart to fear,
And grace my fears relieved.
How precious did that grace appear
The hour I first believed.

John Newton (1725–1807)

First car: Ford Mark II Escort; red/silver two tone; registration YAG 894S; bucket seats inside; 1300cc petrol engine; bad boy exhaust; price £700.

I'm forming a bit of a theory. If you take the bundle of factors that go to make up a person—age, sex, personality, economic status, politics, beliefs, the whole package—then the car is one of the ways these things can be most eloquently expressed in one packaged, physical statement. I know it is not a radical theory, not very surprising or original—it may even be obvious. I've not read one but I'm pretty certain that *GQ*, *Loaded* or even *Woman's Weekly*, for that matter, will have a 'What your car says about you' space-filling article every now and then.

Take my current vehicle of choice: an 04 registration, Mitsubishi L200 four-wheel-drive pick-up. It's practical, hardworking, reason-ably priced and ideal for lugging the straw bales about. Exactly what you would expect a farmer to be driving—with one difference: it's too clean, too well looked after, lacking the dents and scratches that you would expect. It's pristine. And that is because I am a *new* farmer. I've been at it for not much more than one whole year, and I took up farming so late in my life that I'll never completely be a farmer. Both my car and I carry clues to a history that is more eclectic than the 'farmer's son inherits farm and carries on the family tradition' version of events. My car will never completely be a farmer's car and I will never completely be a farmer. See what I mean? Look hard enough and you will see that the car describes the owner more than superficially. Oh sure, you can take the dents out of the bodywork, retune the engine, change a few parts, even re-spray the whole thing, but the car always carries some of its history forward. The chassis remains.

ACN 822V was not a car; it was my first motorbike. I had yet to graduate to four wheels because my age and income constrained me to two. Just as my Suzuki TS50 trials motorbike was restricted to a top speed of 35mph, so I was confined by the sixth form at the Duchess's Community High School in Alnwick, Northumberland. Of course, I'd tried to manufacture a bit of elbow room by stretching the boundaries imposed by the authorities, and my weekends spent scrubbing at the engine block had got the bike closer to 50mph than the manufacturer's handbook would admit possible. But this was a minor triumph, and I knew I wanted to move up from handlebar to steering wheel. It was the same with school. They had stretched the rules and allowed me access to the sixth form common room despite my meagre return of four O Levels the year before, but the last post-Christmas turkey sandwich had barely been consumed before I decided to quit, at the beginning of the spring term of 1984.

Mum was A903 AJR, a 1.3 litre Ford Escort estate. A basic model, no frills, eminently practical and more than enough capacity for all the baggage that a family of three rapidly maturing kids was likely to require. By this stage, my older sister and brother, Mairi and Stuart, had moved on, and while the load-carrying space was no longer quite so necessary, Mum was still available to help her youngest son make those final steps to manhood.

I passed my driving test in Mum's car, so, naturally enough, it was Mum with whom I first tried out the news of my most recent manoeuvre—the emergency stop. Having already told the school that I would not be returning, I broke the news to her, knowing that in effect this was just the last one-hour lesson before the real test. She took it well, recognizing that there was no point in protesting. She expressed her disappointment behind an acceptance that I was old enough to make my own route choice without stopping to ask directions from her or, indeed, anyone else. I was turning into a man and beginning to fit the stereotype. But stereotypes are stereotypes precisely because they do generally fit. So we parked the conversation and she headed for the kitchen and a cup of coffee to await the outcome of the more meaningful examination that I was about to sit.

Dad was in the living room. B554 EVK. A Sierra 2.0 GL estate. A good solid car with a little more about it than the basic L model, but nothing extravagant—nothing special that would turn heads at the traffic lights. It would take a highly trained car psychologist to notice the care that had gone into ensuring that this model was a little better preserved than others of the same vintage. It was not normally clean or polished. Dad was more interested in the practical issues that produced results than in appearances—practical, eco-nomical, reliable, dependable and distinctly lacking in any outward sign of passion. He would need some pushing to get any really startling reaction, but my concern was that my news would be just enough to take him into the red zone.

'Dad, I've decided to leave school and go and get a job.' Hands fumbling for something to do, eyes not sure if they should look at him or the carpet, not sure if I should stand or sit down. Of course, I had rehearsed the conversation many times, and in my own versions his response varied between anger ('Well, if you want to throw your life away, you are not doing it living rent-free here') through resistance ('You are not throwing this chance away; you go straight back to the school and ask them to take you back') to disappointment and resignation ('What a waste'). If anything, I dreaded the last reaction the most. I had always felt that there was a distance between me and Dad, a personal space that we had never quite bridged, but that didn't mean that I was not interested in his approval. Oh yes, his disappointment would have been worse than the fireworks of confrontation.

Be careful, though, with predictions based on stereotypes, because there are surprises to be had.

Acceptance. I had never expected acceptance. Dad agreed with my conclusion that I was not going to do anything at school except endure, and explained that he understood the motivation behind my decision. He reasoned that it might well be better in the long run if I indulged my passion for cars and looked for a degree of independence, and that I should probably find myself a trade where I could earn some money and find some elbow room in which to grow. He told me that when my elder brother and sister had headed off to university, he had given each of them some money from his savings to help them establish themselves in digs. Neither he nor my siblings had ever told me of this bursary. He went on to suggest that he give me my portion and that, as soon as I found myself a job, I could put the money towards buying my first car.

His response, his understanding, marked for me a change in our relationship. Of course I thanked him for the money, and at the time it was the cash that felt like the prize, but as I look back now, I recognize that his acceptance was the real gift. I wanted a car, but I had been searching for acceptance for much longer. I realize now that I have never really thanked him for the way he handled that moment, and I should. It was an undeserved and unexpected reward from a father who had always been there for me, but was showing me for the first time that he had a deeper appreciation of who I was and a fuller understanding of what I really needed than I had hitherto suspected.

You see, I was the youngest of three and, while many may document the trials of the middle child, it is my experience that the youngest has to walk a tightrope between expectation and individuality. My elder sister Mairi was one to whom application brought academic achievement. She worked hard without sacrificing popularity, such that she was elected to become deputy head girl at school. Stuart came next and cruised through O Levels and A Levels. So, when the same teachers encountered number three, they had already mentally filled in my university application forms. Surely I'd be another chip off the same block. To me, the pressure to be another success was tangible, but it was not based on a measured assessment of my own potential. Rather, it was as if my characteristics and talents were assumed, based on those of my brother and sister. It may be that some people would rise to this challenge and use the pressure positively. I chose not to be number three on the production line and opted out. I wanted to be me, defined by my own actions and not by my ability to match others. I jumped off the fence towards the individuality side before I fell off on the expectations side.

At school, I had opted out as soon as I began to understand the nature of the pressure. It was not so much a deliberate decision to make my own impact as a response against the chill felt in the shadows cast by my family. Curricular effort was saved for football, rugby, cricket and athletics. Outside the gates, and sometimes inside them, instead of chasing a ball I spent my fourth and fifth years chasing girls, playing with motorbikes, drinking surreptitious cider and smoking. As a form of rebellion it was nothing spectacular and nothing especially riotous, but certainly enough to draw a thick black line between myself and those oppressive expectations. In effect, I started the process of defining myself by first making it clear who I was not.

The erection of this type of barrier can be dangerous, and Dad's wisdom in accepting me as different was crucial in ensuring that the shutters did not go up on our relationship. In churches they have some jargon to cover this eventuality. They call it 'grace'. I once heard it defined as 'an unearned blessing given to an unworthy recipient'. How strange that my dad should start the process of reconciliation between us by employing grace, especially as, while Mum took me to the local church up to the age of 14 or so, Dad chose to walk the dog along the beach on Sunday mornings. Perhaps these stereotypes aren't all they're cracked up to be.

No, Dad's demonstration of grace (and it seems funny to see the word applied to a man who would be startled to hear himself described as graceful) could not possibly have been learnt from the pages of a Bible or from rapt attention to sermons. I think I am correct in saying that he is strictly a weddings and funerals man— not even an appearance at Christmas, as far as I can recall. These days, it marks one of the differences between us but in those days it was a shared characteristic. As soon as I was able to exercise my own choice, I removed 'attendance at Anglican church' from the Sundays in my diary and replaced the appointment with pursuits associated with an entirely different spirit. Not alcohol—I certainly didn't drink on Sunday mornings. It was petroleum spirit that drove my engine.

During those teenage years, I did have one other brush with organized religion. Brother Jonathan (that capital 'B' is not just because it starts a sentence) was the Guardian (capital 'G') at the nearby Franciscan monastery. Mum had introduced us, although I'm not sure how she knew him in the first place. He was certainly not the media cliché of a cloistered and cloaked abbot and, while he may well have lived a life of dedicated religious observance, my relationship with him was based upon sporting discipline. Every morning, Brother Jonathan would take a rather athletic constitutional, running for three or four miles along the beach and coastal paths thereabouts, followed by a swim in the North Sea. Sometimes I would join him for the running. I'm not exactly certain of the motives at work here. Perhaps Brother Jonathan ran with me as part of his evangelistic duty, as a favour to my mother, or just for the company. Perhaps Mum recognized that while the Book of Common Prayer was not likely to hold much fascination for me, a more masculine and down-to-earth influence might show me a version of the church that was more likely to appeal. I just enjoyed the running and I have always preferred company to solitude.

It was devastating, then, when Brother Jonathan was found dead, having drowned on one of those morning swims. It was my first ever brush with mortality and I recall being deeply shocked by it. Teenagers are supposed to feel invincible, not weighed down with an understanding of the temporary nature of life.

Although I had rejected school, I was not unemployed for very long, and while I was still 17 I was taken on as an apprentice mechanic at Haugh Head Garage. This was the local Ford and Suzuki main dealer, large enough to have six or seven lads working the cars plus a couple of salesmen and a bit of help in the office. I absolutely unashamedly loved it. Working on and around cars, chatting through the new models as they arrived at the showroom, tinkering with the old cars that were dragged in by exasperated owners, bantering with the boys, using my hands, and fitting in instantly—above all, being accepted. The smell and the feel of the garage lingers poignantly in my mind. I can think of a million scenes played out against a background of blue overalls, blaring radio music, tea in mugs, fingernails with a permanent black edge, greasy rainbow puddles and the satisfying clunk of metal against metal. No real responsibility, no real pressures, and a little bit of money in my pocket—my own earned money. Not much, mind you. As a first year YTS trainee, I stuffed 38 quid into my jeans at the end of every Friday afternoon. It stretched just far enough to ensure that when I had bought Thursday night's beer and fags, I still had just enough petrol in the tank of the Escort to get to work on Friday mornings. There is a certain freedom in that. When you can't make any commitments greater than £38, when you have the safety net of living at home, then life can be as simple and straightforward as it is ever going to get. I lived in this uncomplicated way for three years, during which I progressed enough to make me feel that I was getting on, without it ever becoming too much. I wasn't bored and I wasn't looking for any particular change of direction. I wasn't missing anything.

It was A626 BSC that confused matters. An XR3i, what they used to call a 'hot hatch'. A sporty number, probably a few too many miles on the clock to make it a bargain but a car that handled well and was on the wish list of many a would-be boy racer.

Behind the wheel was Ruth. It was a job as secretary-cum-office assistant that brought her to the garage every day, and it was the distribution of wages at the end of each week that brought her into the workshop. On a Friday she would bring her skirt, high heels and small brown envelopes into that very male environment. As she did the rounds, eyebrows were raised, knowing looks exchanged and the odd flirtatious double entendre was slipped into the conversation. Nothing more than that, because that was where the boundary lay and everyone knew it. It was a divide more substantial than that created by the colour of our grimy blue collars. In the countryside and villages, where almost everything revolves around the land itself, there are those who work it and those who own it. I was not politically aware in any meaningful way, but I don't think I or anyone else particularly raged against this system. Those 'with' were envied by those 'without', but there was frequently also an accompanying respect, and everybody knew their place. I was a young, bright, chirpy mechanic and Ruth's brother-in-law and his father were my employers—the ones who owned the garage.

On one particular Friday afternoon, with all the scheduled jobs completed and little more to do than wait for the brown envelopes, the workshop foreman stuck his head into the offices and asked if anyone needed their car cleaning. 'Mine could do with a wash,' ventured Ruth, and I volunteered instinctively. In all honesty, it was a chance to get my hands on the XR3i that made me put up my hand.

Having worked my way over the bodywork, I decided to make a thorough job and began vacuuming out the interior. I've always liked to be busy, to have something to work on, no matter how mundane. Even now, I am at my happiest scrubbing out my own car, allowing my mind to drift over almost any topic but finding security in achieving some small virtuous progress in even that trivial pursuit. As I scraped the head of the vacuum cleaner across the clingy nylon carpets, my head pushed almost into the footwell, backside perched on the sill, Ruth's voice cut across the machine's drone.

'I hope you're making a good job of that.' Her tone was light, jokey, friendly and cheeky. Somewhere in there I detected an element of flirting. I seized this opportunity with my usual alacrity.

'I'll make a better job if you let me drive it back to Alnwick.' I knew that was where she lived.

'Deal.'

Of course, I could not resist showing off slightly as I put the XR3i through its paces on the country lanes, but when we reached the town I circumspectly pulled the car into the curb in front of Ruth's flat. The failing light was robbing the street of its colour, pushing everything towards the grey of dusk. In north Northumberland, just south of the Scottish border, early October is late autumn. There was already a chill in the air as the days shortened, each appreciably briefer than the one before. I rotated the key in the ignition and, as the engine noise died, the ensuing stillness was a heavily pregnant pause.

'Would you like to come in?'

Yet another opportunity in a day that, only a couple of hours previously, had promised to peter out into the routine transition from work to pub via Mum's dinner table. I accepted her invitation.

As it turned out, the cliché coffee was not on offer. Ruth had been packing to move out of the flat over the weekend, so although there were seats to sit on, much of the rest of her collateral was either in boxes or already gone. In fact, mugs would have been superfluous, there being no electricity. So with nothing to fire up the bare light bulbs hanging from the six inches of flex in the ceiling, we sat in the dark and talked. And talked.

It was the kind of talk that sucks up time—vacuums it up, filters it of any extraneous matter and leaves the experience refined, a pure enjoyment. It was the kind of talk that just flows—open and easy conversation, requiring no effort, no pretence, no desperate searching for the next topic, no awkward silences, no deliberate direction into safe or preferred subjects. As it flowed over many and various areas, we discovered more in common that we had expected. Perhaps most significant was that we were both the youngest members of families in which our elder siblings had fitted neatly in with the version of success that our parents seemed to promote. We had both found the need to express our individuality by going a little against the grain. Ruth had rejected her family's involvement with the local church, becoming first a sporadic and then a very occasional presence at services. We talked through the grey of dusk and into the blue-black of night before I headed for home.

Is it any surprise that our first genuine date was to attend a car rally? The Alnwick Motor Club used to organize a night event each year, the Julie Shiel Memorial Trophy. I don't think it happens any more: it is certainly not publicized on their website. It started at midnight, and most of the spectators gathered at the town hall to see the mud-splattered cars arrive at the finish somewhere near four in the morning, having negotiated the tarmac lanes and tracks weaving across the South Cheviot hills.

It was the type of atmosphere I have always loved. Little knots of people scattered everywhere, hugging Styrofoam cups of tea, the air full of steaming breath illuminated by the orange street lamps. The soundtrack was provided by the throaty rattling cough of exhausts and the hum of laconic conversation. I know that as a north-easterner I take pride in our 'salt-of-the-earth' reputation and our legendary friendly openness, our egalitarian ability to chat away to anyone, but I suspect the shared experience of the all-nighter would have removed social barriers in Esher or Egham, too. Everyone at the event was a friend with whom a joke, a greeting or an observation could be shared. Perhaps only the drivers and their crews were an élite as they swapped anecdotes of greasy corners and hidden dips on the route. Ruth and I soaked it up together, chatting with each other. I shared with her my encyclopedic knowledge of the brake horsepower generated by this car or the suspension set-up of that one. The night ended with breakfast, which was al fresco fried bacon and eggs near the finish line.

Given the very public nature of our first night out together, it was a de facto declaration to the people of the area that we were an item. It was too small a community to hope that our attendance together would be anonymous or unobserved. There would have been some idle gossip as the facts were relayed and checked by the interested and not-so-interested parties.

'Did you see him and Ruth together last night?'

'Ruth? Her from the garage?'

'Yep.'

'Are they seeing each other?'

'Dunno. First I've heard of it.'

Against this background of enquiry and, of course, the more direct questioning from my colleagues at the workshop, we played it cool, for a whole week—no longer than that. I don't recall any doubt that something special was developing. Perhaps I was sensitive to the fact that Ruth would have been embarrassed by too much open speculation at work, especially given the presence of family members. I'm not saying we were Romeo and Juliet, but we were moving outside the normal boundaries. Perhaps I was not completely sure that my burgeoning interest was reciprocated. After all, blokes can have a special insecurity about such things. Whatever the reason for the delay, it was the following Friday, with the promise of another brown envelope, before I ventured another invitation—to Newcastle.

For any youngster growing up in a rural environment, the lure of the city is irresistible. By their early to mid teens, every boy and girl has an awareness that there is an exciting, fast-paced, brightly lit world so very different from the cycle of life that is governed by the arrival of rain, the severity of frosts and the price of agricultural diesel. For us, long before any hint of the Tyneside regeneration had brought Newcastle to the attention of prospective students across the whole country, it was the candle flame that drew us from sleepy Alnwick. I asked Ruth if she would like to join me for a night out on the 'Toon', and of course she agreed.

I can't recall all of the details of that Saturday evening, but that is not a standard, bragging reference to the amount of alcohol we drank. I've never really been an excessive drinker, preferring a social pint (lager in those days) to a full-on several-pint session. I do recall that we finished the evening at the Stage Door nightclub. Would you believe, in this age of urban regeneration and frantic rebranding, that it is still there to this day, on Stowell Street, right in the city centre with its blue façade crushed under the weight of a very 1970s-style block of offices. Ruth and I, having squeezed inside, found a table away from the dance floor and again we chatted the night away. We drank in each other's likes and dislikes, hopes and fears, musical tastes and career ambitions until two in the morning, when the club disgorged its clientele. We walked back to my sister's flat, where we stayed the night together.

It was at about that time that my career changed rather radically. I had bumped into an old mate of mine—Richard, who had trained as a chef and then worked as a pub landlord. He had given that up to work in Minories Garage, Ashington. He told me they needed the services of a junior salesman and introduced me to his boss, the garage manager. He reckoned I had enough about me to make a salesman, and who was I to disagree? Let's face it, as the song suggests, everybody's looking for something, and my sweet dreams were of making my own mark on the world. It felt good to be 20 years old and to be the one who had the keys to the company car, before I had the keys to my own front door. In a smooth transition, I had moved up from the budget but souped-up Mark II Escort to a brand new E-registration Peugeot 205 Special Edition.

The car was shiny white, like my collar, which was now decorated with a smart narrow tie and covered by a Burton's suit. I had arrived, big time. I could talk fast, drive fast and burn the fuel that came as a perk of the job. I could look my brother full in the face as I disagreed with him over the relative merits of the Ford Sierra and the new 405, of which I had advanced and privileged knowledge as an official sales representative of the Peugeot dealership.

With salary and commission, I was doing all right. Ruth and

I were still a couple and by that stage it seemed only a natural progression that we would move in together. We found a flat in Alnwick. It did not seem like an especially big move for me: Ruth and I were deeply in love, I was financially independent and we wanted to be together. My family were very passive in the decision and I did not discuss the move with them or seek their opinion on the wisdom of the arrangements. I told them what we were doing and then we did it, and to this day I am not really sure how they felt about it. I am not aware of any significant conversation between Ruth and her family, either, but in their case I am pretty certain they disapproved. Ruth's parents would have felt that to live together before marriage was just wrong. Sin was to be shied away from, to be shunned, not to be lived in. I don't believe they disapproved of me, and indeed I had always felt very welcomed and included by the family. It's just that we weren't going about things and making our commitments in the correct order. Of course, for our own reasons, both Ruth and I were driven towards running counter to expectations, so perhaps no one should have been surprised.

Grace—that word again. This time it was displayed by Ruth's family, who, in contrast to my father, would have heard many sermons on the subject. It is strange when I reflect on it now, but their demonstration of grace is almost more remarkable than his, given that it would have been easier to lecture or denounce. Churches, by reputation, respond to the rule breaker by punishing, spurning, expelling. The local church may often resound to tuts of disapproval on encountering the inappropriate choice or the alternative lifestyle. Had we ourselves experienced that response, it seems likely that we would have been driven to further rebellion. It is almost certain that Ruth's family had to learn resilience in the face of disapproving glances, whether real or imagined. The fact that they responded to me with grace and not rejection is worthy of mention, my gratitude, and reward. I hope, in reading this, they find all three. One very practical expression of their willingness to accept me into the family was the invitation I received to return to work at the family Haugh Head garage as a salesman. It is not quite as emotional as the tale of the prodigal son but, one has to admit, there are some similarities.

I never asked Ruth to marry me. We just grew into an expectation that we would get married. We had (and still have) a relationship built on mutual understanding and an ability to talk to each other. Of course we were living and sleeping together, but the sex came later in our relationship than the friendship. I was 21 and it was the May Bank Holiday in 1988 that became the point at which our informal and largely unspoken expectations became a formal declaration. We were driving to Aviemore and stopped en route in Berwick. While browsing in the window of a jeweller, we decided that it might be a good idea to order the rings. Suddenly, being the proud possessors of a receipt for two gold bands forced our hands.

'Don't you think we had better tell our parents?' suggested Ruth.

I told mine and they were delighted. They liked Ruth and probably knew it was a matter of 'when' rather than 'if'. The more formal occasion was with my future in-laws. With a nod in the direction of tradition that we felt would be appreciated, Ruth took her mum into the kitchen to break the news while I was left alone with her dad. I told him rather than asked, rushing it out as fast as I could. He was great about it, congratulating me and welcoming me to the family. It was a moment of celebration, and we were engaged. The relief that Ruth and I felt was probably something that we had in common with Ruth's parents, who felt that this might be a sign that she was at last settling down and moving from the rebellious to the more respectable.

Ruth's mum never gave up her hope for our salvation. I know now that throughout this time and the following months she prayed for us every single night. When you think about it, that is quite a commitment. Each of us has our own catalogue of major and minor dramas affecting our daily existence. For most of us, as we tire towards the end of the day, losing the energy required for the battle, we seek a little respite in some routine escapism. It might be sport or television or cross-stitch or Monopoly. Ruth's mum took the time every evening to face one of her concerns and, out of genuine love for us, she petitioned God.

Less discreetly and more pragmatically, she also sent us a copy of *Every Day With Jesus* each month, and the little square book of daily Bible readings became part of our routine too. Our Friday night escape from the world was to meet at the local pub for a few pints, a lot of chat and as much laughter. We would ease ourselves into the weekend, wreathed in cigarette smoke, sitting around a crowd of glasses with friends, celebrating a good week of sales commissions or bemoaning the then mediocrity of Newcastle Town FC. Having loosened the hold of the weekday workaday matters, Ruth and I would stroll home to bed. Then, each Saturday morning, we would prop ourselves up in bed and read the Bible notes for that day, chatting over the merits of Selwyn Hughes' latest offering.

For Ruth, I am sure this was a valuable salve against some of her growing concerns. There was a sense of alienation from the norms and standards set by her family that she felt as a deepening emptiness inside. As a teenager, she had quite deliberately rebelled against the family routine of attendance at the Brethren chapel. It is likely that this was more an expression of her dislike for the firm pressure to attend, exerted by her dad, than any strong feelings about Christianity. Perhaps the decision to get married, to become an 'honest woman', was a catalyst for her to begin to consider her stance on other issues. For Ruth, 'to consider' is a verb which is interchangeable with 'to worry'.

Shortly after we announced our engagement, Ruth and I agreed to abstain from sex until our wedding night. Why? I could see that for Ruth, doing things 'correctly' was important. For her, it was another step in the process of reconciling herself with the values her family had implanted in the formative early years, before teenage assertiveness placed a wedge between her and paternal control. Some may have seen this step as retrograde, but the romantic within me, never really far beneath the surface, saw it as a way to heighten the occasion of the marriage itself. Besides, I was madly in love and I found that even lust can be willingly quelled in sacrifice to the needs of my lover. And so, each chaste night we would hold each other and count down the days to our union and reunion.

For Ruth, it was not enough. It was a step in the right direction, an acknowledgment that there was such a thing as a 'right' direction. To admit this is also to recognize that there is a wrong way. She began to feel that she had become the person she had heard spoken about in hushed and disapproving tones during her church attendance when she was a 'good daughter'. She had become a 'backslider'. It was too big a burden. One evening the dam burst, and Ruth's tears burst forth as she pushed the key into the lock of our flat door. It was a Sunday evening and we had just returned from lunch and an afternoon with her family. As the relaxing day drew to a conclusion, we had prepared to go home and, unknown to me, Ruth's dad had asked her if we would like to go with them to the evening service at the chapel. This time it had not been a request or a demand, it had been an invitation, and in it Ruth had felt the weight of her father's disappointment and concern.

I was happy to do anything to support my fiancée, so the next Sunday I dressed in a shirt and trousers and we headed off with her family for the six o'clock service. It was the chapel of Ruth's childhood, a place where she knew she would be meeting people who had known her since birth, who had delighted in her confession of faith as a youngster, who had admired her family unity, who had raised eyebrows as her attendance diminished, who had prayed for her as she went astray. The cost for me in keeping Ruth happy was to endure cold, hard wooden pews for an hour. I didn't have all those ghosts to face. Ruth may have endured the experience feeling that she had made a step towards her dad. I was just bored stiff by the standard Brethren gospel service.

A few weeks later, we went again. I could face an hour of tedium each month as an investment in Ruth's unity with her family.

Speaking at the service this time were an invited couple, Lucho and Lorna Velez. As the names suggest, the pairing itself was something of a novelty in the rural community. He was Columbian, she from the west of Scotland. When they were not speaking in rural churches, they were working as missionaries in Bolivia, setting up children's homes for the street urchins, the orphans, the lost. When Lucho stood up to speak (the idea of women giving a sermon was still a little too radical for the Brethren church at that time), I sat up. This was not the dry recitation of scripture and learnt interpretations borrowed from concordances and commentaries. His charisma and vibrancy lit up the room, filling it with verve and vitality. He spoke from the heart. As a salesman, I knew that nothing convinces like conviction, and as this man spoke I could almost taste his living, breathing belief. I'd never seen anything like this. It was compelling. Whatever I might feel about organized religion, it was clear he had no doubts.

One month earlier, I had been able to leave the church with my preconceived prejudice intact. This time I left with questions, many of which I addressed to Ruth. Perhaps sensing an opportunity, the church started reaching out to us too. I don't honestly know how it was organized, or indeed if it was organized, but we were contacted by a younger couple who invited us to attend another fellowship, this time in Alnwick.

I had hoped to find some more of the fire that Lucho and Lorna had displayed; I was disappointed. The congregation were almost all older than us, used to a regular diet of hymn-and-prayer sandwiches, comfortable with the routine, finding security in it. I don't doubt that they found it nutritious, but to me it bore little resemblance to the salsa and spice that I had found more enlivening. To be completely fair, I must credit the people I met there with a humility and generosity that transcended any interdenominational rivalry. They were almost apologetic as they recognized that what they offered was just not our style. 'It is lovely to see you here, but you might be better off at the Baptist Church,' they admitted.

But there were other matters to attend to. On 2 September 1988 we climbed into the wedding car. I had the certificate in my pocket that formally recognized the identities we had assumed some months before: I was officially her husband and she had changed her name to match mine. It was a natural progression for us. There had never been a proposal and acceptance, just a growing and deepening conviction, and our smooth transition to happy couple had been an evolution. The ceremony was not the start of a new chapter or even a new sentence, but a semi-colon half-nod in the direction of the rules of our families and an agricultural society. We were together; we got married; and so we headed off to Mallorca for our honeymoon, having accepted new titles: Mr and Mrs.

We discovered, as almost all those progressing through their 20s do, that conformity is a gravitational force that is almost impossible to resist. Our next major step was predictably conventional: with the help of the building society we assembled the £27,000 required to buy 54 Cornhill Estate, a three-bedroom end terrace. Having settled in, we decided that we should indeed find out if we would be better off at the Baptist Church. They too had a service at six each Sunday, so one evening we decided to give it a try. As we approached the door, we heard singing and music. It was not the wheezing of an organ or the stilted, regimented recital of hymns, but sounds that we would recognize as music and enthusiastic singing, and it was enough to stop us from entering. Instead we stood outside, slightly confused. Perhaps we had got it wrong. Perhaps there was some special event going on. We dithered on the threshold, half whispering as we wondered what to do. The longer we delayed, the worse it would be to be discovered on the doorstep, and so, slightly scared and very embarrassed, we turned and fled.

It was two weeks later that we tried again, and this time we managed to get inside. It was different. There was real music, there was heartfelt singing but, much more compelling than this, there was love, sincere love. Not just love for God, but for each other and even for us, the two strangers who had wandered in off the street.

At the end of a service in which I found I could not doubt the genuine belief of those in the congregation, the pastor came up to us, welcomed us and introduced himself. Don't they normally head for the door as the last chorus fades and wait there to shake your hand and wish you a good evening? His approach certainly did not seem like a formality; he sought us out and tried to make us feel welcome. Others from the congregation followed suit. I remember Steve and Helen, but they were not the only ones who greeted us. Everyone we spoke to seemed genuinely interested. One or two suggested that they would come and visit us or get together with us during the week. Of course, as any newcomer to a church knows, there is always a lingering suspicion that this is a routine, a rehearsed sales pitch to the potential client, a recruitment strategy. So despite the apparent warmth of the greetings and introductions, as we drove home I turned to Ruth and confidently asserted, 'They won't come and see us, you know.'

The pastor, Jack, knocked on our door one evening that week and Ruth invited him in. We sat down in our front room and chatted freely. As we did, Ruth started to open up until she found herself confessing her rebellion from her family church. We later discovered that Jack was in his element faced with situations like this. He listened, he expressed concern and care for Ruth and, more than anything, communicated a sense that he wanted to support us both as we wrestled with the emotions, questions and search for identity in which we were engaged.

Jack met us in our house and in our situation. What was that situation? We were not unhappy or struggling in any way that friends or neighbours would easily identify. I was doing well in my chosen career: I had found a job in which I felt confident, a job that provided me with reassurance on a regular basis as I closed a sale and earned a commission. We were by no means rich, but ends were meeting fairly easily. We had our working, eating, drinking with friends, socializing routine in which we were very comfortable. We were newly wed and deeply in love. We were just fine. So why had we pursued the church, repeatedly visiting? Why had Ruth just gone though some kind of informal confession with a pastor? Why were we searching? What were we looking for?

Acceptance. Simple as that. I have described myself as being loved into the church, but when I look back over the depth of relationship I had with those most instrumental in bringing me to the point of commitment, it did not speak of trust or friendship built up over any significant period or even any significant relationship. It was purely that they accepted us for who we were. We did not feel judged, did not feel that a rule was being run over us to see if we measured up to the required standards of behaviour. There was no sense that some expectations had been created for us and that we needed to enter a program through which we would be moulded into a preconceived model. We just felt that we were accepted. Perhaps I could better express it in this way: we fitted.

In some senses, Ruth and I had been trying to find a parking space that we fitted for years. When our families and teachers had showed us neat and predictable options, we had instinctively pushed away, only really finding a deepening of relationship when those near us, whether linked by blood or by circumstance, accepted us as we were. When Dad had reached out and endorsed my choice to leave school, when Ruth's dad had stopped offering a preset solution, we made connections that had previously eluded us. And I must admit that, sometimes, the requirement to fit an unfamilar mould was more a factor of our own preconceptions than the reality.

At that Baptist chapel we hit upon a new discovery. We found an environment that moulded itself around us, that flexed and filled in to accept our angular corners and rough edges. It was an environment of security, of grace, of love.

The next Sunday, when Jack made his regular invitation to come to the front to commit to Jesus, I responded. I felt secure and loved enough to stand up in front of all those strangers and new acquaintances, to bare my soul, to cry. In return I found supernatural acceptance and from somewhere I heard Jesus speak to me: 'I've seen this coming for so long.'

I'd not finally fitted into a stereotype and I certainly did not become the clichéd 'church regular'. You could not even tell what had happened to me by a detailed assessment of my car, which even now steadfastly refuses to sport a fish badge. I had simply come home.

Wholly Spirit

They say that God is everywhere, and yet we always think of Him as somewhat of a recluse.

Emily Dickinson (1830–86)

In suburban Kuala Lumpur, the fact that God was involved in everyday life was precisely that—a fact. It was universally accepted, unquestioned. It was as real as air, more evident than gravity, more taken for granted than breathing. Let's face it, every now and then we have all held our breath to see how long we can, or lain awake listening to the gentle rhythmical hiss in and out, actually thinking about the possibility that we might stop. But the idea that getting up, going to school, doing homework, playing in the street, helping with the chores, all happened without the active participation of a spiritual being was absolutely inconceivable.

That belief intruded on even the most basic of daily functions. If I was caught short and needed to run into the forest to relieve myself behind one of the broad, fluted canopy trees, I would stop first, spit three times and then pray that the spirit of the tree would not take offence. I am still not sure what type of revenge a tree spirit with its nose out of joint might exact, but it was better not to find out. In our street, every house had a shrine somewhere. It might be a small room off the living area, or a small alcove, perhaps near the front door, populated by treasured figurines or representations— reminders. There was no choice about believing; the spiritual world was part of the furniture—ubiquitous, universal, omnipresent.

People did vary, though, on the question of what particular variety of god they chose to base their lives on. The majority of our neighbours, like most people in the country, were Muslim. The rhythm of their day was set by the *salat*, the five ritual prayers. On the altars in their houses, there would always be the family copy of the Qur'an, sometimes surrounded by representations of Adam, Ibrahim, Musa, Dawud, Isa and Muhammed (peace be upon him). The Buddhists added colour with their burnt burgundy and sun-bright orange robes. Their shrines were to the Lord Buddha, sitting cross-legged in the place of honour, wreathed in the aroma of the semi-rancid butter tea. There was less consistency in the houses of the Hindus, who might cement paper images of a god to the lintel over their front doors with cow dung. They had the advantage of choice, with Brahma, Vishnu and Shiva well represented. Their statuettes included Naag, the many-headed snake god, and elephants riding mice. Their candles prettily illuminated doorsteps and garden paths during Diwali. The animists did not need the altars, worshipping and fearing the spirits that they identified in the trees and stones and streams of the world around us.

Not that we lived in some rural backwater wrapped in mangrove swamps or rainforest. Ours was like a street from a 1950s council estate—a row of closely packed houses with small gardens. It was a kind of Malaysian version of *Coronation Street* hemmed within the confines of our country's capital city. But our physical separation from the natural world was no barrier against the incredibly pervasive, superstitious folk religion that had leeched into the city from the villages. Like a red sock in a washing machine, it touched all the other religions and belief systems in the machine until everything had that little bit of pink stained into its fabric.

For example, my family were practising Catholics. Behind the little doors on our altar were the china statuettes of Jesus (the same man the Muslims called Isa) and especially his mother, Our Lady. I went to a convent school, I read the Bible, I had seen the *Jesus* film, we went to church, and I had been confirmed. Yet when we experienced misfortune—if we lost money or suffered some other reversal—then my parents would consult a medium in the hope that the spirits might help with a solution. This was not a secretive activity, hidden from their priest for fear of excommunication. It wasn't even seen as something to be confessed. The medium was a Catholic medium, officially sanctioned and part of mainstream religious practice.

It is, of course, hard to know where religion ends and culture starts. We had so many practices and rituals drummed into us that it could be difficult to know which was Catholic and which was Malaysian. Perhaps some were both. After all, our ethnicity had a lot to do with our religion. As Eurasians, our blood was a concoction, a blend of Chinese and European ingredients, the majority of the constituents being imports. Perhaps we had some Dutch ancestry, shipped over with the East India Company that brought so much in return for the rubber it took away. More likely, there was a Latin European strain from my mother's side. Her family lived in the Portuguese settlement close to the fishing harbour, where Catholicism had landed. So it may be that the Holy Roman Church was in our blood, that the superstitions were part of our community, and that our culture was a fusion of both. However our assorted beliefs were assembled, what I might now regard as a series of inconsistencies and contradictions, I then regarded as entirely normal.

It was something from another country, another culture, that jolted me enough to make me look deeper. During my teenage years, America had started exporting its culture to the world, finding films a more efficient mode of transport than ships. Having watched some Cecil B. DeMille-type epic on the life of Jesus, I was so moved by the closing crucifixion scene that I went to a corner of our house and sobbed with emotion. It was the first time I considered that there might be a special depth, something of substance about our religion, that should not be blindly accepted but required investigation. Although I had been labelled a practising Catholic for every one of the 16 years I had been alive, I had never really given it much thought. After the emotional response to the film, the following twelve months became a year of enquiry. Instead of reciting church words as a ritual chant, I began to think about their meaning, asking questions, considering the truths that must lie behind the rules we followed and pondering the implications for my future. I began to try to understand exactly what it was to be a Catholic—what it was that made me, us, different and special.

Perhaps others did not seriously question these things—or maybe they did but they kept it quiet, afraid of what might happen, happier to preserve the status quo of peaceful coexistence. So often, conflicting beliefs have been the source of violence, but despite the diversity I don't recall any particular tensions or divisions between the families in our street. Like any other child, I was often to be found in my friends' houses and it was just as common to be entertaining the son of a Muslim or Buddhist family at our home. It was all pretty friendly. However, children are not always good at understanding the social frontiers that their elders find difficult to cross, and it may be that there were issues to which I was youthfully oblivious.

The post-independence Malaysia of the early 1960s was not that holy grail, a harmonious melting pot. Despite the frequent inter-marriage that had taken place during its modern history, the country was brewing trouble. The indigenous Malays looked with envy and concern at the Chinese population who were becoming more and more influential in the country, particularly economically. The wealthy Chinese used their power to attempt to counter the Malay passion for *ketuanan Melayu*—Malay supremacy—and achieved significant gains in the elections on 10 May 1969. The jubilant Democratic Action Party organized a victory parade, which was supposed to stick to the Chinese areas of Kuala Lumpur. I, like everyone in the city, understood that certain areas were too dangerous for me to frequent—the places where my ethnicity stood out like a white sheep among black wolves. The parade, however, provocatively departed from its published route and took its placards suggesting that the 'Malays go back to their villages' to the poorer district of Kampung Baru. Reportedly there was a lot of offensive chanting from the jubilant crowd.

A retaliatory Malay parade was organized for the following day.

Rumours spread of attacks by Chinese on Malays and vice versa. By 16 May, Kuala Lumpur and the surrounding state of Selangor had descended into anarchy and violence. A state of emergency had been declared. In the race riots, the uniform of each side was skin colour, and I was marked out as belonging to the minority. Many hundreds were killed in the street fighting and, of the several thousand homes that were destroyed by fire, over 90 per cent belonged to Chinese families. The Malays had asserted their authority and those who were not part of the vocal majority became acutely aware of being outnumbered.

I was not at any of the parades and I was not involved personally in any of the violence. That is to say, I was not attacked or threatened directly by anyone. I had friends from both communities and when you know people they look past your facial characteristics, your skin tone, your anthropology. When they don't know you, the way they treat you is almost entirely dependent on those same factors. I was physically unscathed but I saw people I knew beaten—a bus conductor dragged from his vehicle by a group and kicked to the ground; a friend hacked, literally hacked until lifeless. I saw anger and blood and hatred and fear and scars and stuff that I don't even want to try to remember. There were vigilante groups on the streets, no-go areas for each side, burning cars—and seared hearts.

The indigenous Malays reacted out of fear, fear of losing their country. Shaken by the apparent rise of the Chinese and citing the riots, the government drew up the Malaysian New Economic Policy. It was a package of affirmative action in which quotas were set for the Malays in jobs, educational institutions, housing, share holdings in companies and acquisition of commercial property. It meant that government jobs were only available for the Malays, who had mainly come from the fishing and farming communities.

For me, at 17, it meant that my grades at O Level were not good enough. They were good grades, but I was Eurasian and there were far too few places at the pre-university Royal Military College available to non-Malays for me to stand a chance. Ninety per cent of the places were allocated to those who were native to the country. I was not Chinese, I was not the cause of the tension, but I was a victim of the response. I got a rejection letter, and rejection can engender some potent emotional responses in a teenager. The personal consequence of the policy was that I had become a minority, with minority rights and minority prospects. Denial, injustice and disadvantage can make powerful fertiliser for the growth of disaffection and bitterness. I didn't merely believe I had the ability to do well; I had the empirical evidence of my talent in the form of exam certificates. The fact that my ethnicity proved to be the decisive, indeed the only factor in determining my educational career reeked of injustice.

Hatred of injustice, playing fair—very British attributes. My family, along with many others in this ex-colony, had absorbed these attitudes; indeed, we had devoured them and made them part of our own world view. My father had served in the British Army, so as a young man he was indoctrinated by so many moustached, stiff-backed officers in the virtues of discipline, honesty, playing with a straight bat, and so on, and so on. When he left, he took up a senior post in the *Sok So*, the new Malaysian Inland Revenue. Like any of the fledgling administrations emerging from the petticoats of the Empire, the new civil service emulated Whitehall in its structures. My father's job was to set up the superannuation scheme, the equivalent of National Insurance—a system that had at its roots the correction of inequality, being a progressive tax that reallocated a small proportion of the money from the 'haves' to pay for services needed more by the 'have nots'. His career was spent appreciating, serving and building democracy. Perhaps he had tutored me so well in respecting the associated values that I was unprepared for the Asian approach to handling such freedoms and responsibilities, where (in my experience) bigotry, racism, protectionism and corruption were commonplace.

The trauma of my experiences during the race riots, the fear and tension that followed, the sense that I had been robbed of opportunity, and the conviction that I had become a victim of injustice and discrimination left me greatly disillusioned with my life and my environment. Being part of a culture in which the spiritual realm is recognized as an integral part of the physical experience, I quite naturally turned against my God. If he was part of everything, then he must have been part of this injustice. I blamed him. I despised him. I wanted nothing to do with him. In a rage of rejection, I didn't deny his existence, I just asked him to leave me alone: "I went looking for you, and this is what you gave me? Fine. I won't bother you any more in future.' I did something that would have been inconceivable to me and my family only a couple of years previously: I deliberately abandoned my religion and my faith.

Then, at 18, I abandoned my country. Having managed to study for and gain my A Levels, I had again experienced the problems associated with too few jobs being left available for non-Malays. It took me six months to find my first paid employment, working in the offices of the Kuala Lumpur Hilton. While there, I applied for and was offered a place at the London School of Economics to study Psychology. I was determined to shape my own destiny and to escape the system of my country, and to do so I had to take a rather pragmatic approach to the application process. For example, to secure the place at LSE as an overseas student, I had to demonstrate that I had the means to pay the course fees. Clearly my family did not have anything like that sort of money, but I befriended a client at the Hilton hotel who agreed to allow me to show details of his bank account when demonstrating the resources at my disposal. With the offer letter from LSE and a host of other documents, I walked to the British High Commission to apply for my visa and sweated while I waited for the response. Eventually it came, and perhaps my father's years in the service of Britain had counted for something because I was granted permission to enter the UK and study.

For many Malaysians—indeed, for people all across the subcontinent—a British visa was and is a winning lottery ticket. I would have been envied by many, but I did have a brief moment of doubt about my decision. In the intervening time, my employers had recognized my ability and had promoted me to work as an accountant. Then they offered me the chance to go and study in America on a fully paid scholarship, in return for an agreement to commit my immediate future to the company. In retrospect, I probably should have jumped at the chance, with all the financial and career benefits it promised. Perhaps it was the fact that my father had worked for the British, perhaps it was because for years our country had looked up to our colonial administrators, or perhaps it was one of those values of loyalty and integrity that we had learnt from them, but I had accepted the place at LSE and I did not seriously consider changing. I had made my commitment, like a promise that should not be broken. So, rather than being funded by the company, I had to scrape together my own funds for the flight to England. I could not afford a return ticket and I could not even afford a flight by one of the more usual routes. My first journey on an aircraft was courtesy of Aeroflot via Moscow.

The reputation that the Soviet state airline carried was well deserved. Even I could tell that the plane was not in the best shape. It was little more than a creaking pressurized tube staffed by prison warders. In some ways, the attendants were good preparation for my one-night stay behind the Iron Curtain. In Cold War Moscow, the welcome was even cooler. There was no choice of hotel: we were escorted to a grey, threadbare building to which we were confined by patrolling armed guards. That and the extreme contrast with steaming post-monsoon Malaysia—the windy autumn of a September in Moscow—made the whole thing a surreal, dreamlike experience. Eventually, having endured another bout of torture at the hands of the cabin crew, I arrived in London and grasped the meaning of commitment. I had exactly £37 in my pocket and no return ticket. Sink or swim, like it or not, I was here to stay.

The first item on the agenda was to register at LSE and settle my course fees. This was, of course, impossible. I talked fast and earnestly, explaining that I had very little option but to pay my fees in arrears. Fortunately for me, universities like LSE in the 1970s were extremely supportive of students from the 'Third World'. It was almost a liberal form of educational superannuation, and there was an eagerness to spread around the benefits of the facilities. My proposal was accepted and I was allowed to stay, recognized as something akin to an economic asylum seeker.

Second item on the agenda: earn some money. Even in the early 1970s, the princely sum of £37 did not go far, although it would have carried me for several weeks back at home. I got myself a job as a petrol pump attendant (remember those?) dispensing two- and four-star to the motorists of Fulham. I would shiver against the sleet and snow, the cold, wind-driven rain, wiping the November drips that ran down my nose as I pushed the nozzle into the back of a British Leyland Maxi or Mini, then crouched down to the window to collect the cash from the driver. As the window was wound down, I would feel the warm air escaping from the interior and experience another form of economic discrimination. When I went home, huddled in my jacket on the cold vinyl bus seats, I felt keenly the difference between myself and all those who could choose not to use public transport.

In many ways, I had been far more comfortable in Kuala Lumpur, with a home to return to and the support of my family, but crucially I felt an important benefit from being in the UK. As I learnt early in my psychology course, there is a hierarchy of needs. Maslow, the famous industrial psychologist, suggests that when you have food and shelter, your mind turns to the higher issues of relationships and of fulfilling your potential. Back in Malaysia, the chance to achieve these pinnacles had been removed, or so it seemed. In London, although I had dropped down a few rungs to the point where my day was about 'getting by', earning enough to pay the rent and other basics, I actually felt more upwardly mobile. The glass ceiling imposed on my ethnic group, if not completely removed, had been raised, and by applying my talents assiduously I could make it. One day I would be driving a car, working in a position of respect, getting on.

That is not to say that I completely escaped racism. I was a young Asian man, living in a cheap Fulham flat not far from the Craven Cottage football stadium. When Fulham lost, we had our windows broken. I got called 'Paki' on the street and I learnt to avoid the larger groups of supporters on their way to and from the matches. I don't want to overplay the situation, though. I did not feel the same fear that gripped certain ghettos in Kuala Lumpur, and I was so focused on student life and work that the background noise of racism did not interfere with me greatly.

I got myself another job, spending nights pushing the infirm around the corridors of the Charing Cross Hospital, a conveniently short walk from my digs. Then I found a third income, elbow-deep in the greasy brown dishwater of a restaurant. Three jobs were still not enough to enable me to live luxuriously, though. With three Malaysian friends, who were also attending lectures in the hours between blue-collar jobs, I had taken a flat that the landlord had advertised as sleeping four. Once the deal was signed, and without his knowledge, we found another four to join us and split the rent, two to a bed, sleeping in shifts. We would share the catering, too, boiling up large pots of noodles or spaghetti in the small kitchen. Cheap digs, basic food, minimum sleep, pumping petrol, scrubbing plates, pushing patients—pushing, climbing, straining to get on.

I learnt a lot, and not all of it about psychology. Adapting to life in London had its own lessons, some very basic. Take, for example, my first tutorial in ergonomics. In Malaysia, all of the toilets (the ones that aren't trees) are holes in the floor. What do you do when your toilet comes with a seat and a lid? Squatting was what came naturally, so initially I perched with my feet on the rim and adopted the familiar position. It was a while before I worked out that I could sit down, and it took even longer for me to get over the discomfort of actually having to touch a toilet with any part of my anatomy other than the soles of my feet—how unhygienic, and I thought these Westerners were supposed to be advanced! They didn't cover that in the lectures.

What they did cover was three years of general psychology—formation of personality and disorders, psychometrics and sociology, Freud and Piaget. Having completed that course successfully, I had to select a specialism, and I chose clinical psychology for my fourth year. Why? The appeal perhaps lay in the respect that those with white coats seemed to generate as they strode purposefully down the hospital corridors. It is difficult to know exactly how much of my own personality had been developed during those three years as a student in the metropolis, but I had certainly moved on in some ways. I had taken with some verve to the pop culture of the 1970s, styling myself on Jimi Hendrix, complete with an afro of proportions that now seem ridiculous—so big that I used to get bees stuck in it. I strutted my stuff, complete with flares and flowers, around the student parties and into the wards of the King Edward VII Hospital where I had my placement.

It was there, among the starched stiff sheets and iron beds, scrubbed floors, disinfectant and body odour on a male medical ward, that I first met Deborah. For a man in his early 20s, it was difficult to look past the uniform of a student nurse, but of course she had that in common with her contemporaries. The uniform did wonders for her legs, which were great. She was undeniably good-looking, with shoulder-length light brown hair and a glow to her complexion that spoke of outdoor life. She carried herself with a presence that mingled innocence, even naïvety, and personal confidence or maturity, and which marked her out from most of her fellow students.

Diagnosis: country girl from solid, supportive family background. Prescription: more consultations to get to know her and find out more.

We met most often at parties. If you can, think back to the typical

1970s student party. Add a fog of pot and cigarette smoke, a few bottles of cheap wine, dim lighting, arrogant young trainee doctors (almost exclusively male) and impressionable younger student nurses (absolutely exclusively female). For your backing track, choose anything of the time, but especially the Stones, Cream and, of course, Jimi or Eric. It works for pilots and air stewardesses just as well as for doctors and nurses. I had the added advantage of already having graduated with my basic degree and being exotic. I was cool; I knew it. I lived the life, smoked a bit—though never drugs—and drank a bit, although never to the extent of many of my contemporaries. As for girls ('chicks', as I called them then), that was never going to be too much of a problem. However, I found that as other couples danced, sank back into the beanbags or disappeared into the bedrooms, Deborah and I would be soberly chatting the nights away, removed from the drunken promiscuity around us.

I found her intriguing. She did indeed come from the country—Cornwall, to be precise. She was not 'easy' in the way that the girls from closer to the London 'scene' seemed to be, and of course little is more attractive than unavailability. What I also discovered as we became friends was that first impressions could be wrong. While outwardly she carried herself so beautifully, she hid a background that was not at all stable. In her young life she had experienced her fair share of trauma and difficulty, living with her father in council estates and caravans at a time when, despite the liberal social politics, single-parent families were still rare enough to attract attention. The playground can be a cruel place in such circumstances. We talked a lot, grew to like each other, and I found myself wanting to care for her. In the age of free love, ours was earnt.

My first impressions of clinical psychology were also wrong, but in this case I was not prepared to hang around to find out if the attraction would deepen. I began to feel that if I spent much time in the company of those who needed my professional help, I might well end up joining them. I switched specialism and instead trained to become an industrial psychologist. The subject matter was now more about the relationship between the industrialist, the worker and the environment in which both operated. On one hand, there was the controlling dehumanization in a car production plant, where work was obsessively reduced to a series of simple and repetitive tasks in which the worker was simply a machine required to act, not to think. The repressive regimes in some places—the privileged owners' use of brutal 'security' agencies to control the workers and combat the power of unions—emphasized the economic discrimination that seemed to pervade almost everything. On the other hand, British industrialists like Cadbury and Lever, with their benevolent capitalism in Bournville and Port Sunlight, showed an alternative approach. In many ways, industrial psychology was about finding a way to bring into harmony the objectives of those 'with' and those 'without'. I seemed to grasp it more easily and understand its application more readily.

I graduated and immediately found a place with British Gas on a management training scheme—the fast-track. This suited me fine as I was in a hurry to be successful. I think that, when you come from a position of disadvantage, the alternative to submissive acceptance is to grab anything you can get and turn it to your advantage. The need to succeed becomes its own objective and I had become a driven man. I moved from British Gas to Unilver and then on to British Airways, working as a project manager in a joint venture with Boeing to design the interior of the new passenger aircraft, with particular emphasis on the number of passengers that could be squeezed into the new jets before antisocial behaviour resulted. Yes, I am afraid you can blame me the next time you are sitting in economy and tutting as the seat in front of you is tilted backwards until your plastic cutlery and foil-covered Chicken Supreme are dumped into your lap. Later, I took a position with Shell and was seconded to Oslo to work on the design of the accommodation platforms that workers in the North Sea would live on for weeks at a time. Every move I made was onward and upward.

My employers, many and various, rewarded my diligence, my long hours, my appetite and my ability with more money, more responsibility and more training. I was sent to Cranfield School of Management to complete an MBA, to Oxford to gain another post-graduate Masters, and even to Harvard to add the letters 'P', 'h' and 'D' to my name. Achievement, progress, onward and upward. Even without the clinical work, I attained the title of 'Doctor'. I had my car, I had my house in Maidenhead and I had added business acumen to my understanding of psychology. I now wanted a seat in the boardroom. Soon I had it. It was all an adventure in which, having scaled one peak, I would allow myself only a few seconds to enjoy the view. From one lofty vantage point I would spot another summit, higher and more inaccessible, and head for that. How high could I get?

Sometimes my Asian roots worked for me and I found myself on senior committees or appointed to top teams as a token of the company's stance on diversity. Sometimes my ethnicity placed me in the limelight as I was shoved to the front of the photograph to demonstrate how politically correct my employers were. It didn't mean the dividing line had gone; it just meant that the tokenism gave me an opportunity, and I stepped on that foothold as eagerly as any other.

On other occasions, I found the boardroom more offensive and blatantly racist than the shaven-headed Fulham supporters. I recall one chairman of the board being forthright in a way that would be dangerous, inviting legal action if it were in a provable or public context. No matter, I had become double-glazed, triple-insulated against such things. I'd seen race used as a reason to beat people senseless: against that, a few ill-chosen words cause a momentary boiling of the blood, easily cooled by a glass of Chardonnay. Sticks and stones, and all that.

Deborah and I married shortly after my graduation and soon had our first child. The news that she was expecting our second was, in part, the catalyst for a change, a re-evaluation of my work/life balance. I was commuting into central London from Maidenhead every day and working long hours, so that the clocks had to take their annual spring forward to British Summer Time for me to stand even a chance of seeing my house in daylight. Although I did not want to be one of the very first of the downshifters, I did recognize that for my family, especially Deborah, a life away from the ever more crowded suburbs might be better. I began to look for opportunities that would take us to a more rural setting.

It was not long before I found just what I was looking for—a position in an electronics firm in the West Country. It seemed ideal, a chance to move back to a setting that would be familiar to Deborah and also for me to continue moving on up. The Finance Director there was my contact and, after a brief negotiation, I was in, with an offer of a seat on the board and the chance to earn an equity share in the company. There set before me was a chance to complete the journey from shop floor to actually owning a bit of capital, the means of production. It would not have been the end of the road, but it would have marked the achievement of something that would have been impossible in Malaysia, where there were still ethnic quotas for ownership of shares. I would be the outsider made good, earning my place at the table.

We moved to Devon, set up home, and I focused on continuing the success story. I had just got going when the news came that the owners had decided to sell the company. It effectively removed any chance I had of getting a share myself, and it felt as if the carpet was being whipped from under my feet. There was no time to feel betrayed, and typically I responded fast by pulling the top operational team around me and attempting to construct a bid for a management buy-out. But we were too far behind to recover and we lost out to the external buyers. It was another setback, but I had encountered many of those and all had been circumvented in one way or another. I would just have to look for another route. In contrast to London, however, the West Country did not offer many options for the type of employment I needed. It did not seem right for the family to move back to the city, so I decided to set up my own consultancy business. The adventure continued and Pi Management Limited was born. It was 1990.

It quickly became apparent that I was suited to being an entrepreneur and that the problems at the electronics firm had, in fact, been nothing more than a hiccup, nothing less than a blessing in dark glasses. I provided support and advice to senior managers in developing their individual potential and that of their top team. My insight into personality, provided by my psychology training, allied to an understanding of business dynamics, meant that my contribution was immediately valued. Without ever advertising, without ever having to go out and deliberately sell, my order book, workload and company grew, first through my personal network and then through referrals from satisfied clients. In fact, the company doubled in size every year for the first five years. From my base in Taunton, I was running a small but successful global consulting practice, with 200 staff and a blue-chip client list. We had assignments in Europe, America and Asia, sitting at the boardroom table of household brand names. I was flying high, all over the world.

Deborah was at home with our young family, amply provided for. All was well.

Now I know what you are thinking. This is the point where something goes wrong—the bottom falls out of our world; some tragedy makes us re-evaluate our priorities. The sand on which we were building our castle got washed away and, although the situation was desperate at the time, it also provided the jolt that we needed in order to understand some of the more important and ultimately enriching things that we had hitherto overlooked. I'm afraid that this was not the case: after all, this was real life, not a Disney film. The adventure, the progression, continued—although there was one small but significant change. It was not a change to me but to Deborah.

It was difficult to explain at the time, but she quite suddenly became a bit... well, happier. The source of the change could be traced to a weekend visit she had spent with some of our friends in the commuter belt—Chorleywood in Hertfordshire, to be specific. While there, she had been to church with the friends and on her return seemed to feel that she had experienced something profound. She sort of glowed, was a bit more alive and radiant, as if she had discovered the solution to some problem that had been weighing her down but did not have the ability to communicate precisely what this marvellous remedy was. Nonetheless, she was excited to be free of her previous burden and could not help but show it. She started to use one or two words that I had locked away, banished from my lexicon—most notably, 'faith'.

At first I was cynically amused by her new zeal. If she wanted to play at religion, that was fine by me. I had advanced beyond the stage where I needed anything so childish or deluded. Psychology has been described by some as the search for rational explanations for behaviour, the pursuit of 'why'. I'd been trained to diagnose the root cause of this or that emotional and seemingly irrational response; indeed, I had made a successful career out of it. I felt I knew with certainty that this phase of Deborah's would run its course. Perhaps, if I thought it through, I could identify some of the circumstances from her early life that would generate a perception of loss, which attendance at church, prayer and God could appear to her to mitigate. But why bother? It was not doing her any harm; in fact, she seemed altogether happier for it. I decided that if she wanted to play at God, then I was content to let her do so.

Deborah intended to take it all a bit more seriously than that, though, and soon wanted to find a church for us to attend on Sundays. She plumped for the Zion Baptist Church in Taunton and became a regular, occasionally dragging me along when I could find no decent excuse not to go. She started to get to know people there and then upped her attendance to twice a week, with one meeting being what she described as a 'house group'. Once or twice I went along with her to this midweek evening meeting, held, as the name suggests, in the home of one of the congregation.

Initially I was rather surprised. I had expected the regulars, the more religious, to be either old 'spinsters of the parish' or perhaps those who obviously needed something like the church to provide the support and succour they were unable to find in the real world—single mums, unemployables or those with other problems. Instead, the room was full of people who were, well, normal—just like us, in fact. They were mainly professional people, clearly with reasonable jobs and a good standard of living—accountants, managers, teachers and the like. In fact, one of the regulars was a man I recognized as the lawyer I engaged for my corporate work. I had, of course, had several meetings with him and got to know him reasonably well, or so I thought. I had never once suspected that he would be the sort of person who was so committed to the church.

As I sat on the comfortable sofa of a spacious and tastefully decorated living room, sipping decent coffee and listening to these sensible, balanced, educated people talk nonsense about a supposedly loving and caring God, I found that my response was to be deliberately provocative and argumentative. Perhaps I was just irritated by the fact that this stuff was, via Deborah, now beginning to interfere with my life, maybe even brainwashing her into a new and slightly more cheerful person whom I did not completely recognize. One of the key elements in my attraction to her was the idea that I could care for her, but now she seemed to feel she needed more than I could provide. Perhaps it was awakening some of those long-buried emotions that had resulted in me parting ways with God and all things spiritual back in Kuala Lumpur. I'm sure, if I had been able to practise some form of astral projection, hovering up near the ceiling so that I could analyse myself from a safe distance, I would have diagnosed something of the sort.

Of course, in middle-class British social gatherings, you don't voice aggression in any direct or obviously threatening way. Instead, playing by the rules that the English fully understand, you confront in a subtle and challenging way, presenting a façade of interest and engagement but in a way designed to highlight the flaws, the weaknesses in their position. And you do it with a smile. So I discussed, even argued with my hosts and the other group members. I asked awkward questions, challenged perceptions, attempted to highlight inconsistencies or contradictions. All the time, I acted out the part of a intelligent enquirer, seeking to get to the crux of an intriguing philosophy. There was no strategy: I just wanted to be disruptive, awkward. I wanted to shore up my own position of certainty, reinforce it and perhaps at the same time show to Deborah, if no one else, the folly at the vacant core of their belief system. Surely, sooner or later, they would realize that the king was in fact naked, his new clothes an elaborate mass illusion. He was not a loving God; he didn't care about people. I knew that from bitter experience.

I became infuriated that none of this performance seemed to work. I certainly failed to dent the resolve of the churchgoers, or even that of Deborah. I'm not sure if they saw through my behaviour for what it was and just humoured me, or whether they were convinced by my act and were pleased to have someone doing the full due diligence, checking out their story before making a personal decision. Whatever it was, they debated with me without losing their faith or their tempers. At home with Deborah, I became more belligerent and at one point threatened her: 'You are going to have to choose between your faith and our marriage.'

Of course it was unreasonable—irrational, even. Totally unfair. To appease me, Deborah agreed that she would reduce her involvement with the church, become less active—and for a while she did, or so I believed. What I know now is that she continued her activities but without my knowledge. At home she would head off to the utility room with a bundle of washing and load it into the machine. Then, masked by the whine of the motor and the churning of the drum, she would pray in earnest, speaking out her requests and petitions. I've no doubt she prayed repeatedly for me and for a change in my heart and attitude. If the opportunity presented itself, perhaps if I was away on business or working late, she would find a way to steal along to the house group meetings in secret. Perhaps, while she was there, she shared her concerns about me with the group; perhaps they all prayed together for me.

'Would you like to come to church with me?'

It was the corporate lawyer, phoning me at home one November evening. The invitation came with no warning and I was caught so completely off guard that I agreed.

The next Sunday, I joined him at the church. It was (still is) one of those modern, almost triangular church buildings, probably planned in the '70s, with no spire or tower, built of red brick and wood, and with one of those long sloping roofs that almost touches the ground on one side, and tall rectangular glass windows. Not exactly beautiful or inspiring—more functional and practical. It is not actually in Taunton itself, but on the other side of the motorway, in the village of Creech St Michael. The setting is so peaceful that outside, if all is quiet and the wind is blowing from the west, you can hear the rush of cars on the M5, almost a mile away. When the music stops inside the church, you can hear the occasional rush of a train heading south to Exeter or north and east to Bristol, and then on to London. As I wriggled uncomfortably on my seat, somewhere towards the back of the hall, I envied the passengers on the Inter-City express, rushing past and away from this backwater. While all around me people were clearly caught up in the service, enjoying the singing, murmuring their approval of prayers, raising their hands above their heads, I was bored. I glanced at my watch, trying to guess roughly how long a typical service might be and how much longer I would have to endure it.

Hang on a minute, something unusual is happening. A woman—not one of the professionals up the front, just a member of the congregation—is standing up and speaking. She's telling everyone some message from God, or at least that is what she claims it is. No one is shushing her or tutting or motioning her to shut up and sit down. There is no one smiling sympathetically at her, humouring her as one would a misguided child or someone with 'difficulties'. Amazingly, the others seem to be paying close attention to her, some watching her closely, others with their eyes shut as if praying. It's as if they really believe she has a message from God, like a modern-day prophet or something. As if that type of thing really happens these days. They do! They really believe they are listening to God, who has chosen some middle-aged woman as his mouthpiece.

Amazing.

Wait.

What is it she is saying? She's talking to me. No, not to me, she is talking about me. She is not using my name, but it's me she is talking about, describing my life.

Look.

Yes, 'look'.

I can see what she is saying—actually see it, like a video. I'm only half hearing her words now, but I am seeing my life being played back to me. This is my life. I can see myself, the adventures I have had, all I have been through.

Hang on again, it's coming to an end. Who is this here? It's Jesus. Yes, I am sure it is Jesus. He is standing in front of me and he is pointing ahead along a path. He's not actually saying anything but I can just feel him telling me something. No, he's not telling me, he's inviting me. He is saying that this is not the end; it is the beginning. He is promising me that the adventures to come will make what has happened up to now seem trivial. He's telling me there is so much more.

So much more. So much more.

She stopped speaking and I opened my eyes. I was on my knees, my cheeks wet. I had no memory of leaving my seat but there I was on the floor. I sniffed, wiped away the tears and awkwardly pushed myself up and back on to my seat, head down. I hardly dared to look up. Surely everyone else must have noticed what had happened to me. I was confused, of course, but also slightly embarrassed. In that terribly English way, my lawyer friend sat still next to me, looking ahead, pretending everything was completely normal.

I went home and told no one—not a soul. Partly I was isolated, up there on my high horse. I had created a position in which I had been deliberately dismissive of anything spiritual in my own life, and I had publicly denounced this 'born again Christianity' nonsense, so I had no one with whom I could discuss in earnest my sudden and profound religious experience. I couldn't talk about it and I couldn't stop thinking about it. In the middle of an email I would look up from the computer screen, my eyes focused somewhere in the middle distance, running the events of the previous Sunday over and over in my mind. In meetings I would find that, as others chewed over a problem, I would be tuning them out, reducing their voices to a blurry background while I again thought about that final frame in my life video, with Jesus pointing up the path that snaked into the future. Much as I would have loved to dismiss it, I couldn't. It had been so real, so very real.

At the end of the week, I phoned the pastor of the Zion Baptist and introduced myself.

'Ah, yes,' he said, 'I've been expecting a call from you.'

Once I had got over the shock of that, we chatted briefly and then arranged to meet up. I explained what had happened and, to my relief, he didn't look at me as if I had lost my mind. In fact, he acted as though it was indeed perfectly normal. Very special, of course, but nonetheless quite a reasonable thing to happen. He suggested that we go and see the woman who had spoken out the prophecy at the church. On the way there, he sought to prepare me, to help me understand what was going on. He explained that the woman, a well-known member of the church, had given a prophecy on several occasions and that her opinion was reliable. He talked about it in the same way we might have discussed the veracity of Michael Fish's nightly predictions of the next day's weather.

When we arrived, the woman showed us into her living room and made us a cup of tea. With the pleasantries out of the way, she took a notebook out of a drawer and flipped to the most recent entry. She explained that God often spoke to her and that when he did she had a habit of writing down what she remembered for future reference. Then she started to read back what she had written the previous Sunday.

It's the video again.

Someone has pressed Rewind and then Play, and again I am seeing my life in technicolour. It is exactly the same as it was in the church—the same sense of adventure, the same sense that all that has happened up till now is just preparation, just the prologue. Yes, there he is again—Jesus. He is still pointing up that path, beckoning to me with his eyes, inviting me, urging me to embrace the opportunities to come. Offering me something...

She stopped reading and this time I was kneeling on her carpet. I was crying again. I opened my eyes and the pastor and the prophetess smiled at me. They had explained nothing to me, but I had come to a place of understanding. All those years ago, traumatized and embittered, I had rejected God, abandoned him. Now I realized that he had not abandoned me. He had been around all this time, invisible to me, waiting for the right moment to reveal himself, to explain that he had something in mind for me. He was offering me a journey of more progress, more adventure, more excitement than I had already experienced. In a flash of insight, I realized that a decision to follow him did not require that I give up my life. In fact, life with him promised a whole new dimension, new depth and interest. It was a chance to move on to another plane, another level, to break through a barrier and live a richer and more fulfilling life. It was an offer I couldn't refuse. Within a month I was baptized.

Before that Sunday, I had seen life as a series of progressions, something linear, always moving on, achieving more, getting to a new place, achieving the next step. In some senses, of course, that is true. I have moved forward a great deal and, since my commitment to follow the path Jesus had been indicating, things have progressed even further. My business has continued to develop and grow and be successful. It has taken new directions and I've had new and exciting opportunities that would never have been possible without being born again.

In one sense, however, life has been circular. I have returned to that place where the spiritual dimension is ever present, where God is as real and tangible in my everyday life as the food I eat. Like a kid in Kuala Lumpur who expects to encounter some manifestation of God behind every tree and under every rock, like my parents who would seek the counsel of someone spiritually sensitive whenever misfortune struck, I now wake each morning with a sense of spiritual awareness and expectation. Each day feels like a childhood Christmas present, waiting at the end of my bed to be unwrapped. It is thrilling as, each morning, I start with a question that I expect to be answered as the events of the next 24 hours play out: 'What will God do today?'

Just good friends

Surely you desire truth in the inner parts; you teach me wisdom in the inmost place.

Psalm 51:6

Shouldn't the day you publicly confess your faith in Christ be a memorable one? I'm sure it should be one of those moments that define you, that mark a dramatic change. Take mine. It had been arranged in such a way that a senior member of the religious hierarchy was present, not to mention a few hundred contemporaries and their parents. A special venue had been prepared, even spruced up for the occasion, and there were speeches and music, the latter performed by a choir that had been practising for weeks. I'd even been preparing myself, taking a number of lunchtimes to talk through the key issues with a chaplain and a few others who were also expecting to make the commitment. With all that, you'd expect some kind of crescendo—a climactic experience as I triumphantly broke through into a new realm of existence—but actually, I don't remember it very well at all. I recall a little about the event but it is all a bit vague. I can really only sketch in some of the details and half guess at others. It's a bit like trying to recall what I had that morning for breakfast: it was almost certainly cereal; it may well have been cornflakes. Why is every aspect of the service not etched into my mind? Because nothing more significant than eating breakfast happened—not as far as I can tell.

That was not particularly a surprise; I wasn't expecting anything. I'm not even absolutely sure why I went through the ritual of Confirmation at school, although I suspect that the reason had something to do with the fact that my next-door neighbour's son had already done so once he had turned 13. I think my parents had developed an acute awareness of the rituals and ceremonies that were the 'done thing' in the circles in which they operated, so they suggested that I go through those particular motions as a declaration not so much of any particular faith as an affirmation of my family's membership of suburban professional society. So, with freshly pressed white shirt and grey suit, I would have taken rehearsed steps to the front of the wood-panelled great hall where the bishop, probably an old boy of the school, would have led me and about 15 others through the Book of Common Prayer liturgy before laying his hand on me.

It was all very symbolic but, although I had attended the classes designed to walk me through the precise Anglican meaning of the jargon ('salvation', 'redemption', 'incarnation' and the rest), I had experienced no internal 'transformation'. My impression of the other pupils who attended the school Christian Union was still that they were a bit weird, and the ceremony did not bring me into a new position of sympathy or understanding. I recall with delight the indignation that the chaplain once caused them when, during an RE lesson, he countered a very literal interpretation of Genesis by describing the book as a 'Hebrew fairy tale'. I rather warmed to him after this, especially as I had the impression that he wanted to provoke debate and discussion rather than a blind adherence to the prescribed textbook version of events. It's an approach to authority that I have always appreciated, even emulated.

My previous experiences of church had been a mixture of ritual and respectable social obligation. During my primary school years, I had been delivered to the Sunday school of the local Anglican church. Each week we listened to Bible stories and collected stamps depicting those stories, before leaving the church hall to march across to the main building with its pillars and polished brassware, incantations, bells and smells. It felt like a glimpse into an adult world, the Communion a ten-minute taste of a ritual known fully only by those fully grown.

My parents, only occasional attenders, would join me for

Christmas where they would dress smartly and endure the fire-and-brimstone, hell-and-damnation sermon of the vicar. Having determined that his style was too direct and aggressive for their taste, they compromised by only sampling the Midnight Mass each year. It was for them a social event, and when again the vicar dropped his 'P's and 'Q's and used the opportunity of fuller pews to challenge his audience, my parents made their excuses. They eventually transferred their yuletide allegiance to a nicer, softer, friendlier, altogether more comfortable and less challenging Presbyterian congregation. No one likes to be made to squirm in their seats, especially at Christmas.

I think that, for my parents, their sporadic attendance at church was just one example of their desire to be part of the social class and community to which they were very happy to belong—and only a very small example, at that. More regularly they held and attended dinner parties, and more prominently they became involved in the local amateur dramatics society, with regular rehearsals building towards the climactic opening night of *Iolanthe* or some other Gilbert and Sullivan performance. It seemed to me then that everyone in the neighbourhood went to watch, and certainly, in the days preceding the opening night, the talk in our house and on the telephone seemed to be of little else.

I can see now that this may only be evidence that most of my parents' friends were involved in am-dram or were supportive enough to pay for a ticket but, to my childhood perception, for that couple of weeks every six months, our entire domestic world revolved around light opera. I recall my dismay during the nights I was obliged to watch my mother in a supporting role while my dad worked away somewhere off stage. Even then, I regarded them as more amateur than dramatic. The ham was not only found in the sandwiches, *sans* crust, that the cast shared after the last night. The usual leading man, Carlo, could sing pretty well and, being half Italian, provided some Latin exotica, but the rest were very clearly the housewives and accountants of a north-west London suburb enjoying a moment in the footlights.

By day, Dad was a manager in a central London branch of the National Westminster Bank. It was certainly a very respectable, professional position, which had provided an elevation from the days when he and my mother got married and had to live in one room of my grandparents' bungalow. Born as the son of a policeman, and thanks to the social mobility of post-war Britain, Dad became white collar, house owning, middle class before I had made it out of short trousers. Solidity and stability were together the basis for a very happy family life. Beneath the hem of my shorts were knees that were grubby from scrambling around the woods at the end of our road, or sunburnt after summer weeks spent on the beaches of Dorset or South Wales or the Isle of Wight. Dad helped us build dens and stuff multicoloured Alum Bay sand into cheap glass ornaments. On weekdays I would walk to my primary school, Mum would head off to work as a secretary, and Dad would commute into London to work at the bank. We were respectable and happily so. As I think about it, there was perhaps a hint of regret about my mother, a sense of loss in choosing to be a wife and a mother rather than pursuing her own talents and carving out her own career, a whiff of missed opportunity—but no bitterness. My family was stable, supportive, happy, secure.

My parents encouraged me to apply for public school and were, understandably, very proud when my results proved good enough to be offered an assisted place. They had only to glance across the fence at our neighbour's son, who had failed the same exams, to be reassured that I had done well. Unfortunately for them, it was not well enough for a full scholarship, meaning that although I had a great opportunity, there would be a significant additional financial burden on the family. Middle class did not mean an excessive income. Each year, Dad would sit down and work through the family finances, constructing the budget and allocating my mum her weekly housekeeping allowance. It was always a time when he was more tetchy and tense than usual—a time when money pressures spilled over into other conversations. With the additional burden of school fees, even discounted school fees, my parents would have to make sacrifices.

Being good, supportive parents who wanted the best for me and my brother, they made those sacrifices willingly. I can only imagine what Dad felt when, having somehow squeezed the regular outgoings to match the monthly salary, he received the list of equipment required for my first day at public school. Tradition and a restatement of middle-class values were very much part of the curriculum: for example, the uniform was a grey suit to be purchased from Harrods. Given the rate at which eleven-year-olds grow, an expensive tailored suit is hardly the most practical or economic solution, but my parents dutifully took me into the West End to kit me out. I suspect it was a month when Mum had a little less on which to run the house, or one that made a dent in the carefully reserved savings.

School was taxing for me too. Not academically—I was far too lazy for that. Natural ability carried me into the top 20 per cent of most classes and I was not inquisitive enough to wonder how much further a bit more application could have taken me. As a consequence, I drew little attention from the teachers, performing well enough to avoid arousing any special concern but not promising results that would enhance the school's statistics and consequently its reputation. What I found hard was to be removed from all that was familiar and placed in an environment for which I had not received any preparation—a place where the rules, expectations and terms of engagement were different from those of my home.

I started as a 'turd', the unimaginative name for the new intake who joined the third (say it with an Irish accent) form at the school. None of my friends from primary school had made it into my new seat of learning with me. The majority of them shifted relatively seamlessly and as a bunch to the local state school, jostling along the pavements as they walked the ten minutes or so it would have taken from our road. If I had bumped into them, the uniform would have marked me out as an exception, but I was long gone before they grabbed school bags and headed for the door. My daily journey as a day boy took between 60 and 90 minutes, involving a walk to catch a bus to catch a train to walk in from the station. It was as if I was exported from my country of origin each day to a foreign land, where each evening I was refused permanent citizenship and deported. I had a passport and a visa but residency was never to be granted and, if I am honest, I didn't really see the point in seeking asylum.

My peers funnelled into the school from a variety of backgrounds. There were those who had gained full scholarships and were clearly extremely gifted and driven to achieve sporting or academic excellence. Then there were those who paid full fees, often not nearly so bright but coming from privileged backgrounds. A number of these boys were from overseas, coming for the cachet of a British public school education. I can't say I really identified with any of them especially, and being a day boy in some ways made that harder. The social élite of the school were the boarders, who, being forced to live in each other's pockets, developed a certain camaraderie and mutual support out of necessity.

Belonging to some of the other easily identifiable groups merely marked people out as soft targets for the inevitable bullying. The Jewish boys and foreign students took the brunt but no one was exempt. There was Richard, who I would count as one of my companions, a Polish boy who I recall once being dragged to the 'bogs' for a vicious kicking. I tried to avoid getting picked on by staying out of the way, but it didn't always work. I was once cornered by an older group who painted me with varnish, although I don't think there was any especially witty metaphor intended. The varnish was probably just a convenient way for them to express some of the spite and aggression that will always ooze to the surface when teenage boys are cooped up together in sufficient numbers.

Chicken or egg? Is the peculiar environment of the school created by the teachers who, by and large, control the activity there, or does that type of environment attract a particular brand of teacher? My form teacher was passionate enough about English to teach it well, with enthusiasm and interest. However, he was also keen to share his enjoyment of French art-house cinema, inviting pupils to stay behind and watch some of his collection. I think I recall that he left quite suddenly. In Maths I was relieved to have sufficient aptitude to avoid too much attention from the master. He employed humiliation as his chief weapon, dragging pupils out to the blackboard where he could take any lack of understanding and enlarge it to make the poor unfortunate look foolish and pathetic in front of the class. When he didn't have time for this sophisticated form of torture, he would hurl anything at hand across the room in anger. There were PE teachers who turned to the slipper at a moment's provocation and a History teacher who turned the subject into a shopping list of dates and unquestionable facts from which interpretation, imagination and interest had to be eradicated.

In response, I ceased to care, even using a History exam to express my indifference by filling the answer paper with facetious comments that I thought witty and, as a consequence, twice failing the O Level exam. I became an unremarkable pupil and, although I am now officially listed as an 'old boy', I don't find my name in any of the lists the school proudly publishes on its website.

In fact, the school seemed to lose interest in me when I opted not to sit the Oxbridge entrance exam, noting that I would not be improving their percentage of pupils going up to Oxford or Cambridge as reported in the prospectus. My parents did not react strongly to this decision, either. It was as if, by getting to public school, I had achieved a great deal and, by being the first in our family to qualify to take a degree at any university, I had done more than enough. It didn't especially matter to them which university it was. Their attention seemed to have turned very much to my younger brother who, instead of applying to my school, had opted for the ten-minute walk to the local grammar school. At 13 he had refused to go through the process of Confirmation against my parents' wishes, for which he earned my respect and envy. While I was keeping my head down and making as few waves as possible in my school, Derek was making quite a splash in his. He was popular and good at sport, excelling at rugby where he played for the 1st XV as well as London Welsh and Wasps colts. There were even whispers of international selection. He was our family's favourite.

I've not said it explicitly but I am sure you will have assumed it: my school was single sex. I went through puberty in the company of several hundred other adolescent boys, being forced to share baths after PE. It was clear that school was not going to provide me with the social and personal skills I would need in dealing with that rarely encountered life form, the woman. My parents were not the types to help redress this learning deficiency, either. If anything, they were turning me remedial. My mother was a passionate, tactile extravert. At parties and even in the social gatherings I was permitted to attend, she could often be quite flirty. However, my parents' prudish reticence to talk about anything that might lead to a mention of 'it' left me with the impression that while there was such a thing as sex, it was embarrassing and awkward and should be hidden away, denied.

Derek, on the other hand, was getting his education at a co-ed school and was racing ahead of me in some subjects. He even invited me to a few parties and tried to give me a leg up by encouraging some of his girlfriends to take an interest in me. I was not resentful of this. I was grateful for the opportunity, although not always exactly sure how I was supposed to behave in such circumstances. Salvation came in the form of a holiday job.

Some friends of my family ran a small hotel in Lyme Regis, a private establishment, big enough to have a swimming pool, a bowling green and a games room for table tennis and similar rainy day pursuits. When full—which was for most of the summer— it would house around 60 holidaymakers, mainly family groups having a week or two at the classic British seaside resort. After my 14th birthday, I was invited to go and work there for the summer holidays, waiting on tables in the large dining room and working as a general hotel dogsbody. From the very first time that the idea was mentioned, it felt like an invitation to explore my limits and develop my own understanding of the world in which there were girls, games and contraband gratification. For my parents, it was something of a gamble but probably a deliberate strategy to give me a little bit of rope, with the added security of their friends to keep an eye on me.

At the end of my first week, I gave them cause to question their judgment when the proprietors phoned to report that I had been thrown out of the Lyme Regis Conservative Club for being drunk in charge of a snooker cue. As part of my initiation, I had been taken there for a frame or two of snooker by two or three of the staff who arrived from Hartlepool for the summer season. They were in their late teens and early 20s and no doubt thought that taking a fresh-faced youngster out for a drink would create its own entertainment. I have always been big for my age so getting served was not especially difficult. However, holding the drink down was more of a challenge. I was immediately threatened with an early return home, but fortunately I was given another chance.

I quickly formed a partnership with a 19-year-old student teacher called Dave, who spent his long summer holidays waiting on tables in the hotel. He became an adopted elder brother and supported me through the ascent of a steep learning curve. Little by little, I shed my reserve. With each passing week my cheeks reddened less when I hovered around the daughters accompanying their parents on their regulation fortnight in the Dorset ozone. With Dave's example to spur me on, I began to push my own personal envelope, exploring boundaries.

Teenagers don't seek to understand their limits of alcohol capacity or decency; instead, they start by learning what they can get away with and how they can use their charm and wit to excuse behaviour that steps outside the adult norms. So, of course, with cider at 20 new pence a pint and wages in my pocket, I spent almost every night out exceeding limits. On one occasion I was dragged home by Dave and a few others, directly through a cow field, arriving back at the hotel in such a state that there was nothing for it but to be thrown into the swimming pool to wash off the worst of the muck. So a summer passed, much of it foggy in a hazy cocktail of Newcastle brown ale and Dorset cider. Once or twice, the boys would also pass some pot around and I indulged in the rare experiment. At school, the drug of choice was speed, consumed with startling intensity by a number of the more dangerous characters. I had stayed clear, not fitting into that particular clique and not finding them at all attractive. However, the casual and very occasional use of soft drugs came as part of the relaxed summer package, excised of any mystique.

Each summer thereafter, I returned to the south coast for my holiday job, and each year Dave returned to resume our partnership. It was not just substance abuse on the curriculum and my feet were not the only part of my body that I was finding. Often hunting as a pair, Dave and I went in deliberate search of a little companionship. We would develop a routine, starting on a Saturday when guests would normally arrive—changeover day. Pinned up in the kitchen would be a list of guests and their table allocations for the dining room. Shoulder to shoulder we would run a finger down the list, looking for names preceded by 'Miss' but with a surname in common with a 'Mr' and 'Mrs'. Once found, we would manoeuvre to make sure that we were allocated those tables when serving the first evening meal. From there, as long as we had not picked out a spinster sister or a toddler, we had ample opportunity to offer to introduce the young ladies to the delights of the town—in the interest of genuine hospitality, of course.

This was the precursor to a series of back-to-back holiday romances, some of them resumed in subsequent years. Each evening would follow a similar formula, starting with an invitation to one of the local pubs or clubs for a drink. With inhibitions suitably eased, we would wander as a small group along the famous curving stone

Cobb weaving around the harbour, or hop over the groynes stretching down the beach and into the sea. Eventually, with the sun below the horizon, we would return to the hotel, walking across the cliffs along the Dorset coast path, pausing for an embrace or prolonged and urgent fumbling and kissing. Sometimes the inhibitions were not so much relaxed as completely eradicated, and it was not uncommon for things to degenerate to a little late-night streaking around the hotel gardens and through the corridors. Fantastic fun.

I was aware that Dave and the others recruited from the north-east went a good deal further than I did. If I represented the forces of conservative home counties reserve, my older colleagues seemed to do their best to exceed the tag of 'likely lads' that was applied to almost any young man with that accent. My mother, letting slip the veil of innocence, once asked me if I used my time in Lyme Regis to 'sow my wild oats'. I'm not sure where oats came into it; the other staff members were just wild, wringing dry every opportunity for hedonistic enjoyment.

Dave and I may have worked as a pair, but I sensed that our motives were different. This was perhaps illustrated by our annual dalliance with two sisters. He would hook up with the elder of the two and, before long, they would be on their own, going all the way. That's not to say he exploited her: she was clearly as up for it as Dave. But for Dave this was serious business, as if his entire year's fun had to be had in six or seven weeks before he descended into a world in which all that sustained him was the thought of the following summer. I was left with the younger sister, who dressed to demonstrate her rebellion and her adoption of feminist principles. I have always respected and enjoyed the company of those who stand for something, who make a deliberate choice not to conform, so we would spend our time talking. That's not to say that we did not enjoy the odd kiss and cuddle—I was only human, and a teenage human at that. It was just that, for me, it was only a holiday and I was happy to take the fun as it came, not really needing to force the pace.

Among the staff, there was one other exception. Like me, he was a family friend of the proprietors, not recruited via an agency from Hartlepool. Tom was a couple of years older than me, completing his A Levels, and I found him impressive. He was quiet and private. His discretion did not seem to come from shyness but, paradoxically, from a certain confidence. It was not that he was a saint but, when he involved himself in the general horseplay, it was on his own terms, withdrawing when he felt his own thresholds threatened rather than allowing the momentum generated by the pack to make his choices for him. Behaving in this way without outwardly pronouncing any judgment on the likelier lads ensured his popularity.

I did not draw any conclusions at the time about Tom's beliefs. My experience of religion was one in which normal life was put on hold for a set-piece performance that had a lot in common with my mother's sorties on to the stage. The idea that a belief structure could impact a person's everyday routines had not really occurred to me. I regarded Tom purely as a character worthy of respect. Perhaps what he did for me was to confirm the developing sense that there was a good deal more to life than surviving school and then playing through the summers. Neither provided the depth that I wanted. I felt there must be more to life than that. Tom finished his A Levels and went on to study theology.

Having passed my O Levels and moved on to sixth form, I was capable of a little elementary life trigonometry—a simple measurement of the depth of my existence. With my holiday fun being no more than light relief from a school routine that I did not much care for, life was a little shallow. The depth I missed was roughly equivalent to the distance between two opposites—Dave and Tom.

It was during those last two years at school that I got to know Marius as a good friend and had a first brush with another dimension—that of spirituality. Marius and his family were Persian and members of the Baha'i faith. When invited back to their house after school, I was touched by the impression I got of a quiet, almost saintly family who had a genuine belief that soaked through every area of their lives, like the rosewater-honey syrup in the sweet, nutty baklavas his mother used to give us with tea. She would pray over us whenever we left the house and, rather than being weird, it felt more like a gracious gift.

Marius was quiet but good fun, and when he was given a Triumph Spitfire for his 18th birthday and we drove it first to Paris and then on to the south of France over the following summer, it certainly contrasted with the Lyme Regis experience of previous years. It was teetotal fun, Marius being a strict observer of rules and his faith frowning on alcohol, but I remember a lot of laughter. He was quite a contrast to Dave and provided evidence that, far from the starched and building-specific religion of school chapel, adherence to a code and a genuine spirituality was no barrier to enjoying yourself.

When I arrived at Reading University, the first item I unpacked in my hall of residence was my stereo, along with my *Genesis* albums. Unloading the contents stuffed into his Mini and carrying them into the room next door was Dean Taylor, a tall, handsome, scruffy agricultural student. The first box he opened contained his coffee filters. It was the beginning of a friendship forged in very late-night chats, very, very strong coffee and dodgy music.

In many ways, Dean was a typical 'agric'. He and I strapped our legs together with three others for the rag week beer race. I remember him throwing a mate's bike into a tree, just for a laugh. But through our late-night conversations, and as we spent time together, I discovered that he had a line he would not cross—a strong moral side. For example, he was completely faithful to Louise, his childhood girlfriend. This was in stark contrast to many of the other students. Two of his close friends—the smooth, well-dressed Steve and his partner in crime, Nick, with his unruly mop of blonde hair and Worzel Gummidge wardrobe—openly worked their way through the female population of the campus. They would frequently try to encourage Dean to join the marathon, but he laughed it off, managing the difficult trick of keeping his distance without appearing at all judgmental or pious.

I'm not sure that Steve or Nick ever even noticed me in the corner of the room, sipping the coffee and with my hand up, keen to volunteer for active service. Louise occasionally visited Dean for a weekend, and when I met her I could see why he was slightly in awe of her. She impressed me, mainly with her strongly held views about a series of ethical issues that I had never even considered. There I was, studying food science, and she was challenging me on the fairness of the trade that brought the filter coffee to our mugs. I enjoyed being stretched and pushed to consider new ideas by someone who was thoughtful, confident and open enough to question the status quo.

I'd not applied the same rigour to my selection of university or course. I chose food science largely after becoming fascinated by the rather flippant suggestion of one of the chemistry teachers that salmon sandwiches could one day be made out of petrol. It was that modernist view of utopia in which technology would provide the plastic-wrapped solutions to everything—a very appealing concept to the *Thunderbirds* generation. When I made enquiries as part of my UCCA application process, the admissions administrator at Reading wrote back asking if I might be interested in a BSc in Food Science and Food Economics. The variety appealed, as much as the ease with which I could secure a place. Indeed, in return for placing the course at the top of my shortlist of five, I received an unconditional offer.

There were seven of us on the course. The neighbour of one of my fellow food scientists was Ruth. She was fantastic. Short, with delicate features and a cloud of soft brown hair, a beguiling soft Northern Irish accent and a bubbly personality combined to make her an inevitable target for almost every bloke in the halls (not to mention the fact that she danced better than anyone else). However, it was also fairly clear that she was unobtainable, being very definitely a strong Protestant Christian, something that she made no secret of but equally did not push on people. I spent a fair bit of time with her, even inviting her home to my parents' house. I'm not quite sure where I thought we were going, but Ruth was absolutely the type of girl that you take home to meet your parents. She was good enough to let me down gently during a walk in the woods near my house, where I had built camps in my childhood. We had gone there so that I could do the thing that young men do when trying to be romantic—showing off the haunts of our early years and the special places of our adolescence. A trip to Lyme Regis might have been a next step. Ruth had a different agenda, though, explaining that nothing was going to happen between us, and she did it well enough that we remained friends without too much awkwardness.

Quite naturally, when a large group of people is thrown together, intersecting circles of friends form, some that endure and others that come and go. Some are based on shared pursuits, such as being members of the table tennis club; some are created through more formal structures, such as being part of the same course or seminar set. These types of friendship rarely endure much beyond the structure that holds them together, despite the best of intentions. The most enduring of the circles is the one based on a pure enjoyment of each other, for no other reason than mutual respect and attraction. As I look back at my Reading days, I see the common and defining characteristic of all of my key friends as being an unconventional spiritual depth and integrity. Undergraduate life can be a pretty shallow existence of doing just enough to get past an exam and going on to the next party, but most of my friends seemed somehow able to float above this peer pressure tide, to choose which elements of the life would be acceptable to them and which elements would not. I found this integrity impressive. I have always been intrigued by those who, because of some principle or belief, refuse to conform. Wedded to this, I admire the ability to question and, out of that questioning, to hold views based on an ethical or moral standpoint rather than accepting the norm. Finally, and crucially, this refusal to conform has to be genuine. The people I liked did not take their principles and create a high ground from which they observed life in a detached way; they were very much part of life, able to enjoy themselves as much as, if not more than, the rest. They were fun-loving people, comfortable with sensuality but not controlled by it.

Quite unexpectedly, I bumped into Marius on the campus. Despite being good friends during sixth-form days, we had not kept in touch after school and I had not even known that he was at Reading. He invited me along to a meeting of the Baha'i Society, a talk on the principles of the faith. The presentation explained their unified field approach to religion, prepared to borrow from almost any religion to create a non-offensive stance. I responded very much to the welcome and the hospitality. They were very, very nice people but I remember thinking, 'Wouldn't it be nice if it were all that simple?' I never once went back.

Ruth, Dean, Anna and Stuart were all part of my core circle of friends. Stuart and I intersected with the table tennis club and I knew that Stuart also crossed over into the Christian Union, where he was something of a key player. Ruth, the Ulsterwoman, and Anna were both strong Christians. I now know that Dean and Louise were both Christians but at the time I hadn't realized it. So it seems that there was one other defining characteristic in that circle, with me as a notable exception. It is to the credit of the others that I didn't notice.

Then there was Elizabeth. Tall and good-looking, she ticked all of the boxes, even the faith box that I didn't know about. In truth, she was someone I saw as being out of my league, so it was going to take some extraordinary courage to ask her out—and at university courage comes from Holland. I staggered up to her at the end of the annual beer race during which I had been strapped to Dean and a couple of other mates, and, being somewhat worse for wear, I popped the question. She said, 'Yes'! I can't quite believe it, even now. Alcohol may have given me a belief that I stood a chance, but it is rare for a man to look like a better bet drunk than he does sober. In such dubious circumstances, and with a level of mature discernment that normally characterizes one-night stands, began the first long-term relationship of my life.

It was wonderful—for two terms. She was beautiful, interesting and fun to be with. We talked, spent a lot of time together, both with friends and alone, and we had a very physical relationship within boundaries that she imposed. Elizabeth would not entertain the idea that we would have sex together and, although I would have been delighted to go further, I did not especially push the issue. Of course, we would be locked in an embrace and in the back of my mind I would be wondering just how far it would go. We would reach the threshold, but the line was clear in the sand—often redrawn but always in the same place, and never crossed.

I very much enjoyed being part of a recognized pair for the first time. I did not enjoy my first experience of break-up.

She ended it. There was a serious, looking-at-the-floor, hand-holding conversation. It was nothing about me. The relationship had just reached its sell-by date. It had been good but it had no future. Better to finish now than to carry on and risk it turning sour. She explained and justified. I tried to act in a mature and rational way, nod my agreement, agree to be friends. I did not agree, though, and all I wanted was to cry, to hide or to do something to get her to change her mind. I did none of those things and we parted.

No doubt, in normal circumstances, the ache would have slowly passed and maybe in time we would have been able to become friends again, but it suddenly got acutely worse. Within days of our break-up, Elizabeth was with someone else. Of course, it could have been her own rebound, an attempt to plaster over the disappointment of a failed relationship, but it was awfully fast. What if she had actually met him before she had split with me? What if the split with me had been the effect and not the cause, that she had freed herself of me precisely because she wanted him? What if her explanations had been excuses and expedient lies? It would probably have been better not to ask, to move on, but in the heat of rejection they were questions that demanded an answer, and I was going to get one.

I stood in the corridor outside the door to her room, pausing for a moment to compose myself. Should I be angry and demand answers or should I be righteously dismissive? Did I want her to confess or just feel a weight of guilt equal to the mass of my hurt? I can't honestly remember because then, through the door, I heard them together. The architects of student halls don't have the preservation of the residents' modesty as a primary objective, so the noise was barely hampered as it came to me through the fire-resistant door. Although not an expert campaigner, I was not a complete novice and I knew exactly what those sounds signified. Forbidden fruit, denied to me, was being enjoyed. She and I had been together for half a year and never got that far, and half a week later someone else had charged across the line and it didn't sound like Elizabeth was putting up much of a fight. My planned controlled knock at the door became a banging with my fists; my rehearsed accusations were replaced by shouts of bitter rage and indignation and humiliation. It burned my cheeks, stung my throat, pricked my eyes. Goodness knows what would have happened if Elizabeth had opened the door, but she was busy. She didn't let me in.

At times like that, you need your mates, but it was Elizabeth's best friend who stepped up. I knew Anna, and I knew that she was another of the circle who had a strong Christian faith. She was also one of those people who was capable of being serious and playful, warm and with depth, so when she came to join me as my partner at our last Reading Summer Ball, I was pleased. I like to dance the night away but I also like to sit and chat into the small hours. We danced a little first, then enjoyed some earnest conversation and, with inhibitions relaxed through claret and Merlot, we ended up back in Anna's room. She was pretty tactile and again I found myself in the embrace of someone who would go so far and no further.

In the following few weeks, we had many late-night conversations. The subject of God and faith recurred but without any strong conclusions. These conversations didn't only happen with Anna but with a few others, too. In hindsight, I must have driven my friends mad with frustration, being prepared to ask questions and listen to the answers, and yet making no response. Anna, in particular, seemed keen to invest time in working through the issues with me. While we were never in a full relationship, in the way I had been with Elizabeth, we did spend a lot of time together. I even went to church with her a couple of times. It was almost as if Anna could see that something was happening to me, that my awareness and interest were developing and deepening. If something was happening, it was invisible to me. I was interested in exploring topics of substance, and clearly something that had such a bearing on the behaviour of people I respected could not be completely ephemeral, but I think I probably regarded my interest more as intellectual stimulation than real searching. It was fun to explore.

That autumn, having graduated with the minimum of effort, I found work as a trainee tea taster at a brokers based in the City of London. I lived back at home with my parents and emulated my father with a daily commute into town. At the same time, I noticed the first evidence of something churning away beneath the surface. The seeds that had been patiently planted by my student buddies had fallen into a moist, rich compost—a combination of a soul searching for a place to belong and an enquiring mind that was finding answers in the lives and patterns, more than the conversations, of friends I respected.

St Helen's Church now lurks beneath the famous London 'Gherkin', that chequered, bullet-shaped tower designed by Norman Foster. In the days when I first went along, the closest landmark would have been the Bank of England, placing it almost equidistant between Fenchurch Street and Liverpool Street stations. Every now and then, I would take a chance and slip out to sit among an eclectic congregation for the lunchtime service. The hard wooden pews were dotted with pinstripe suits, outnumbering the students and academics who also made the midday effort to attend. 'Him we proclaim' begins the motto at St Helen's, and Dick Lucas, the vicar there at the time, did plenty of proclaiming. The architecture resonated with the other buildings of the financial district, with huge fluted stone pillars soaring towards the vaulted roof. It was the sort of building that commanded hushed respect when first entered, but Dick would shatter the silence with sermons full of energy and passion.

I can't say that I agreed instinctively with everything he said, but I did respond to his conviction. I was suspicious, though, of what appeared to be simple answers. My experience of life was already sufficient for me to realize that neat solutions are rarely complete. It was the way my university friends lived that had had me asking questions, and it was the vibrancy rather than the content of the message that kept me coming back to ask more. It was slowly, slowly dawning that the key issue for me was not necessarily the need to tease out all the answers to the theological questions presented, but the impact that Christianity could have on me as a person. I didn't want to become a blind observant, one of those types from whom I had always shrunk. Those I liked and respected were clearly able to have a more substantial foundation to their lives and the associated stability, without surrendering the ability to think for themselves. I began to realize that I wanted to join the club, and that I would have to accept Jesus as the route to finding the same assurance for myself.

Anna had invited me to a New Year's Eve party at her parents' place in Godalming. I turned up with a real sense of expectancy. That was, I suppose, nothing unusual. The dimly lit lounge, the kitchen and the dining room were all filled with people who had been anticipating the party since the cold turkey sandwiches of Boxing Day. For those of us too cool and mature to derive a great thrill from a Christmas Day spent with family, TV and mince pies, the festive season built up towards 31 December. Wine flowed, music blared and people occasionally glanced at watches as they counted down to the centrepiece of the evening. Laughing reminiscences were shared by undergraduate friends who were now becoming dispersed in pursuit of fledgling careers. This gave way to dancing, giggling and the odd romantic encounter, punctuated by refill visits to the crowd of bottles and cans. Glasses were charged, the noise of conversations swelled and people started making rapid plans for a conga in the street or a circle of Auld Lang Syne or who to share a midnight kiss with. At the centre of it all, there was Anna the hostess, with an almost endless selection of people to talk with, laugh with, dance with. Eventually midnight came and with the transition from one year to another there were the usual cheers, clapping, kissing, singing and more drinking.

I was experiencing my own personal and intense sense of approaching climax. I needed to speak to Anna. Seizing her at a moment of opportunity, I explained to her that for almost twelve months I had been building up to this moment. During the now finished year, we had spoken a lot, often late into the night. She had patiently explained things to me, held my hand through moments of crisis and tried to support me in my time of need. I told her of my visits to St Helen's and my emerging sense of conviction about Christianity. I told her that I wanted to make a commitment. Maybe it was the tendency of a new year to encourage the consideration of fresh starts and new resolutions, but I knew definitely that this was the moment. She was incredulous, mainly at the timing.

'Does it have to be now?'

She was clearly torn between helping me to take a life-changing and important step, and the fact that she was enjoying her party. She had, after all, given me plenty of opportunities before. Somewhere about one in the morning we went to a room in the house to get away from everyone else, and there, sitting on the bed and to the accompaniment of muffled music and laughter, we prayed together. It was a fairly simple and short prayer in which I dedicated my life to Jesus.

Just as in that moment of ritual confirmation at school, nothing whatsoever happened. I felt no different and there were no incisive flashes of insight—instead, just a slight sense of relief and anti-climax, to be followed by a vague confusion. It was not dissimilar to that moment just after midnight at any New Year's Eve party, when the focal point has been reached and no one is quite sure when the party itself will actually end.

'So what happens now?' I asked.

'Go and talk to your local vicar.'

It may just have been the second worst bit of discipling I have ever experienced.

The local vicar himself was responsible for the worst.

'Can you come back another time?' On being asked to help a young man with his new faith, he told me firmly but politely that it was not a particularly convenient time to talk. Anna had been reluctant but at least she had dragged herself away from the party.

I had walked up to the door of the vicarage on my way home from work. It was probably a deliberate strategy to do it this way; if I had gone from my home, I may have had to explain to my parents where I was going. I had not thought to phone ahead or arrange an appointment, so my knock on the door was unannounced. The man who opened it was the same man who had driven my parents away from the church with his fiery sermons. Other than that, my only experience of him had been as he officiated at the 8am Sunday morning service to which Mum had occasionally taken me after my confirmation. My impression then had been of plenty of kneeling, half of the service being chanted or sung, and a vague sense of false humility. I'd probably shaken his hand a few times on the way out of the door while exchanging a few insincere pleasantries.

I'm pretty sure he did not remember me. I don't know what his reason was for sending me away. He could have been busy preparing another one of those intimidating sermons, or he could have been already in deep conversation with another needy parishioner.

Perhaps he was just watching *Top of the Pops*, and thought to test my resolve.

I was serious. Two nights later I returned and perhaps passed the test, because I was shown into his study. Given my previous experience of him, I was not sure exactly what to expect. We were clearly generations apart, but to my relief I found a listening ear and a genuine willingness to understand. I explained that I'd made a commitment, a heartfelt one, but that I'd felt nothing. I'd had countless serious conversations about the Christian experience with friends who had convinced me of the existence of the spiritual realm, but when I'd taken the plunge, nothing had happened. The example of the lives lived by those friends, more than the words they used, had been such that doubts about the rewards available had not surfaced. Instead, I had become concerned that the problem was with me. For example, was it pure coincidence that all of my most meaningful conversations had been with women? I was certainly interested in more than just their opinions. I had tasted a little sex and I enjoyed it. I wanted more. Perhaps someone with that type of appetite was not worthy of the sort of religious, spiritual experience that purer characters could attain.

The vicar listened sympathetically. He explained that he had been an army chaplain and as such had a wide experience of the earthier side of human behaviour. Mostly, however, he just listened, and as he did I got no sense of the judgment I feared. Instead, I felt reassured that I was not an evil exception but actually quite normal. As I spoke, I was able to rationalize that my Christian friends had a number of things in common. They tended to have longstanding relationships with partners to whom they were faithful. They were confident in their convictions, enough to resist a good deal of peer pressure. They seemed to be at peace with themselves. They were rounded people and, as a consequence, they were attractive. By and large, it was from this foundation that they were often able to resist the temptations that faced them, rather than being immune to them. The occasional slip in some ways proved this, and the ease with which they recovered from these lapses only emphasized their sense of security.

I like to work things out for myself and, as my explanations bounced back from the walls of that study, I began to understand that there was nothing about me that was stopping God from bestowing his gift upon me. Instead, my own misconceptions and misguided guilt were preventing me from accepting it. I wanted from the vicar some reassurance that my interest in sex was OK, and he provided it. More than that, he provided me with the forum in which to reason out my view of the world and to understand the source of my slightly blurred vision—an upbringing in which a healthy discussion of sex had been absent and through which I had developed shame about my own perfectly natural urges and appetites.

I walked home in the dark through the local park. As I did, I felt a real sense of elation. No, I felt more than that. It wasn't exactly peace. It was an inner calmness, a state in which I was cleared of the turmoil of confusion and conflict and left with a central reassurance, a security, a wholeness. *Shalom* would be a better word. For the very first time, I knew with confidence that I was his, a child of God. This time, something actually had happened.

That 'something' has stuck with me. I've grown and developed in my understanding of my faith without having to give up my enquiring attitude, and in doing so I have seen how belief in Jesus Christ can be at the core of the confidence and balance that characterized the lives of my friends. Several of those relationships have endured the changes of location that our various careers have required. I've travelled widely and been an interested observer of believers in many different gods. I've been an active member of several churches, and I've especially enjoyed working with the younger members of the congregations. I love their open-minded approach to Christianity. You see, although I've found *the* answer, I still love honest questions, and those who ask them. The Jesus I have met, the God I worship, seems to appreciate an honest challenge, too. May I never stop seeking to understand.

Spur of the moment

All growth is a leap in the dark, a spontaneous unpremeditated act without the benefit of experience.
Henry Miller (1891–1980)

For me, it was a spur-of-the-moment decision. I don't mean that it was carefree or especially impulsive. The moment will always be special, but there was no warning, no sense of climbing a crescendo in the days or even hours before. Looking back, of course, it stands out clearly as a high point in the undulating topography of my life, but one where the ground rises steadily towards it. It was not a snap decision, despite the absence of obvious build-up. In retrospect, it is possible to see the myriad contributing factors, experiences and emotions, thoughts and fears—some many years earlier, others almost contemporaneous, but all converging to produce the spur that finally pushed me over the edge.

The lump of rock, cold hard grey, sloped down into the black water of Windermere. I hugged my knees and pulled my fleece jacket tighter around me. The zip was already up as far as it would go and I could feel the cold metal against my nose as I pushed my chin further into the collar's protection. The dry cold of the Easter air gave the sky clarity, and the absence of moon permitted a view of the Milky Way, a pale smear wiped across the double-black sky. The ten-mile stretch of Windermere, a dark marble strip flecked with the stone-chip reflections of stars, reached from just below the soles of my boots all the way to Ambleside. A few electric lights could be seen, even though the pubs had been closed for hours. Behind and above the town there was a discernable line where the night sky butted up against the heights of Fairfield and the other fells, dusted with late spring snow. Framing the lake were the wooded slopes of the east and west lake shore, darkest of all.

There are some moments, just before a commotion, when everything is suspended. The new leaves stretching out above me were motionless. Directly opposite, the road leading down from Gummer's Howe was silent, undisturbed by cars taking the scenic route back from Kendal or returning from the real ale served at Strawberry Bank. One huge collective breath was held.

Only four days previously, this moment would have been impossible, or at least highly improbable. True enough, I'd arrived at Grange-over-Sands railway station feeling a mixture of nerves and excitement, but that was in anticipation of the week-long assessment. The minibus of the YMCA Lakeside Outdoor Pursuits Centre had been waiting for me and, as I threw my rucksack into the back, it had become obvious that two or three of the other alighting British Rail passengers were also being interviewed. The minibus driver, satisfied that he had collected all the candidates arriving on this particular train, had slammed the side door shut and pulled out of the small car park. During the half-hour drive past Newby Bridge and along the narrow undulating road to Lakeside, there had been brief introductions and stilted conversation as we weighed each other up. They were, after all, likely to be my competition for the available jobs, advertised as 'Vacational Instructors' for the busy summer season.

Soon after arriving at the centre itself, my kit stowed in the dormitory, I stood on the tarmac volleyball court with about 40 other hopefuls who had been invited to try out for the 20 or so vacancies that would fill the June–September break enjoyed by most students. The staff of the centre put us through a series of icebreaker exercises and briefed us on the programme for the next few days. The week was designed partly to assess our technical capabilities in instructing the core activities, such as canoeing, climbing, sailing and orienteering, but also partly to evaluate our suitability for living and working in a close community. For this latter purpose in particular, we were organized fairly randomly into groups that would work together for the rest of the week—that is, if you believe in 'random'.

I think it would have been fair to apply the adjectives 'arrogant' and 'cynical' to my attitude about many things, and especially about any selection process. I'm tempted to excuse this attitude as an effect of being rejected by the local grammar school many years previously, despite easily scoring above the qualifying standard in the optional 11+ exam. It seems that the decision rested on the fact that I attended the Sunday school of an evangelical church rather than that of All Saints, the parish church of respectability. It appeared that being Anglican was preferable to being happy or 'clappy'.

At eleven years old I had already begun to learn that it is not what you know but with whom you mingle that counts when it comes to being chosen. This view had hardened over the following ten years so that if, on that first day of the selection process, you had asked me how the applicants had been allocated into their various groupings, I would have had a ready theory. My assumption was that, having looked through the application forms, the Personnel Manager would have used key indicators such as educational achievement, university or polytechnic, not to mention the passport photo clipped to the top right-hand corner, to form stereotypical images in his mind. He would then have placed 'Probables' together, giving them the chance to shine, while the 'Possibles' would have had to do something exceptional.

As a consequence of this belief, I had already taken the precaution of lying on my application form. Not whoppers, of course. I was too smart for that. I'd merely stretched the truth in a number of places in the manner not unfamiliar to Miss World contestants. Let's face it, an interview is a beauty contest, and I was not above expressing my interests as 'working with children' and 'helping others', when 'drinking' and 'having a laugh' would have been more honest. For example, when given the opportunity to 'tell us something about yourself in up to 300 words using the space below', I'd invested four of my allocated words in the phrase 'I am a Christian'. To me it meant that I was not Muslim, Buddhist or Moonie and I went to a CofE primary school, and I'm not sure I was especially aware of any other meaning. I'd used the phrase mainly because the centre was run by the Young Men's Christian Association. I was young, I was male and, although two out of three ain't bad, I wanted to maximize my chances. It might just have been what was required to get me into the 'Probables'. I did not really consider that Providence might have taken a hand.

The first of the week's events was to be an overnight bivouac on one of the upland areas nearby. Having assembled the required kit, my small team of six or seven was given the grid reference for our intended campsite and bundled into the minibus to be driven to the drop-off point. There was June (or 'Ollie', as she preferred), Dean and a beautiful blonde Kiwi woman called Greta. There must have been two or three others whose names have long since gone from my memory. I do recall that we fairly quickly found our location for the evening. We were all reasonably experienced in hill walking and camping, so the basic navigation presented us little problem except to agree on who would take the responsibility. Initially, our high degree of cooperation and mutual support was designed to impress, to get the ticks in the right boxes on the assessment forms of those evaluating us. We were aware that we were interviewees, so a degree of acting was inevitable. I believe I would not have been the only one making the inner calculation—balancing the need to demonstrate that I knew which way to hold a map against the requirement to show good team-player characteristics. As it was, Greta did most of the route finding. After a basic meal, there was little to do but chat away the twilight hours until we were tired enough to climb into the sleeping bags and plastic bivvy sacks. The talk served to deepen our introductions as we started to share more personal information.

Of course, I cannot now remember the precise details of the conversation, but I am pretty sure I would have offered a sanitized version of myself. I know that on a later occasion, Ollie described me as protecting myself with a 'beautiful suit of armour', and I have no doubt that I would have covered up fully in such a delicate environment. After all, first impressions last, even the false ones offered in pretence.

I would not have told them that Luke, one of the students with whom I shared a house in Bristol, called me 'Burnside', after a character in the ITV soap *The Bill*. This epithet was in honour of the fact that, in common with the TV character, I did not appear to care much about anyone or anything. If Luke had been slightly less creative, he would simply have used an alternative two syllables, beginning with 'B'. It was not that I did anything especially bad, but it would have been a comment on the manner in which I went about the regular student routine of drinking, womanizing and occasionally attending lectures. Basically, I would do almost anything for a bit of fun, and if that meant that someone was picked on for the evening because they were overweight or had a Black Country accent or had just messed up in their exams, then that was fine by me. I did not set out to target specific individuals; I was more opportunist than calculating. However, in trying to get a laugh I would use any convenient stooge. Of course, you and I both know that it was another suit of armour, covering my own insecurities, but I don't suppose that made it any easier to handle the barbed tongue and acid comments for any of my many and various victims.

I think most people believed that I was very confident and did not really care what others thought of me. Strangely, or perhaps obviously, the opposite was the case. I, like many, wanted to be seen as cool and sharp and fun to be with. I was acutely aware that I was not naturally endowed with the poise, good looks or charisma to make this happen automatically. There are some people who seem to glide into a room or a conversation and become part of it as if the whole situation had been brewing for the sole purpose of their arrival. I tended to hang back, observing from the edge of a room, waiting for someone else to make a first move towards me, awkwardly hoping for an opening that often would not come. I never made the first move for fear of making a fool of myself: I was too afraid of the embarrassment of refusal.

I believe I was not unique in handling this type of situation by deliberately picking on others, boosting my own self-image by emphasizing the characteristics that made someone else even less part of the herd. They didn't have to be negative traits. There was sometimes even more reassurance to be had in taking down a tall poppy, in twisting their prowess with assignments, assignations or athletics. The important thing was that they could be laughed at and identified as being more abnormal than me. What I can't quite understand now, though, is why I persisted with this conduct as a tactic. Who would gravitate towards someone who could easily be running them down the moment they leave the room? I think I knew the folly and failure even then, but the behaviour was pro-grammed in, impossible to stop.

Another item I would have neglected to mention to my new teammates was Jenny. From the age of 15, I had been pretty consistently in some relationship or other, moving fairly rapidly from one girlfriend to the next. In contrast to most of my contemporaries, however, it was only recently that I had broken my duck, so to speak. Jenny and I had just started sleeping together, both first-timers. When it did at last happen, it had been fairly anticlimactic for both of us, and I am ashamed to say that for me it was immediately followed by a lack of interest in her. It was as if our relationship had been all about getting us past that hurdle and, having achieved that particular objective, there was no special reason to stay together. I was somewhat surprised to notice this coincidental change in my emotions. I had genuinely believed that sex was the next step in the deepening of our desire for each other, a marker for our growing commitment. I was disconcerted to find that it turned out to be the last step before a dead end for my personal commitment.

I am sure I was not the first to make this naïve discovery, but Jenny had yet to make it. I'd hidden my declining interest, putting off the onerous task of explaining that it was all over, perhaps trying to put distance between the decision and the act that had precipitated it. I did not want her to feel used, partly because it would not have been true. It had not been a premeditated plan. As a consequence of our experiment, I had come to realize that physical union was not enough on its own. I guess Jenny was about to learn that men can be Burnsides. It is safe enough to assume that this new discovery was not shared around the campfire that first night.

No matter how comfortable the ground, how warm the sleeping bag, or how tired you were the night before, you always wake early on a bivouac. Our newly formed team, fresh with new insights into each other's characters, was up with the birdsong. Our initial movements were all about getting the stiffness out of joints that had been separated from the hard ground by six millimetres of foam. The night had been cold and cloudless. We breakfasted on muesli with rehydrated milk, choosing to ignore the tins of beans and mini-sausages, mainly because nobody was keen on carrying dirty pans or washing them. Our beds were quickly rolled away and we were ready to go, with the sun still not showing above the trees.

As we assembled by the shore of the small pool of water, no more than 100 metres across, Ollie took a photograph, a print of which I have seen many times since. I bet she still has it in a scrapbook somewhere to this day. It shows a clear blue sky mirrored in the polished surface of the water and framed by the birch trees. To me, it is also a reminder of the freshness and perfection of the morning. Nature was reflecting my sense of promise. I'd found that I was genuinely enjoying the company of my new friends, for that is what they were becoming. Our group had already started to develop a sense of identity that was inclusive and, for me, this positive belonging was liberating. There was good-natured banter, of course, but no need for a scapegoat. I could feel a wholesome quality in these new relationships, not based upon the exclusion of anyone but on the shared experience. It was more than that, though. I'd camped out on hundreds of occasions before, and shared more intense outdoor experiences, without this same feeling. I think it was in some part due to the fact that these were entirely new acquaintances, with whom I did not carry any metaphorical baggage. Our relationships started as clear and cloudless as that morning's sky, clean and with the promise of a day to be built together. Mostly, though, I think it was just that I liked them from the first, and, amazingly, I actually felt that they liked me.

The next two or three days continued to go well, full to the brim with laughter. As a team, we built a flimsy raft on which we barely completed the marked-out course. Other teams fared worse, and the inability of our team to win the race carried with it no sense of failure. In the rock climbing it quickly became clear that Greta, despite being about five foot four inches tall, was by far the queen of heights. Unusually for me, this was not a source of irritation. I always was, and probably always will be, more competitive than is entirely healthy—a trait mostly inherited from my dad, whose genes seem to have a disproportionate influence when you consider that they are technically only half of me.

I remember Dad, throughout my childhood, as an achiever, excelling in almost everything he did. He rose from the working-class roots of post-war Peckham, through National Service and apprenticeship as a glass decorator, to become a senior manager of a major company, living relatively comfortably in the home counties. As with most things, he was successful in arresting the decline in his parents' and grandparents' fortunes, bouncing back up through the class divide. I lived very much in his shadow, aware that I was not as talented in most areas and without his very definite charisma. When Dad was called for jury service, his election by a group of strangers to be the foreman was inevitable. Similarly, in later years when he took up golf to stave off the boredom of retirement, it was just as certain that he would become the captain of his club's seniors.

I should have been envious of him but I never have been. I remember a friend of the family once trying to get a rise out of me by telling me that I was just like my dad, and my response being to puff my chest with pride at the recognition. No, my competitiveness was not born out of bitterness. Bitterness is birthed in negativity and jealousy, and I was never jealous of Dad. It was the urge to prove myself worthy that was at the root. I was always failing the standards he set, never feeling good enough, never quite making it, always second best. When I played for a junior football team in Bracknell, Dad would trump any achievement with stories of representing the armed services in friendly matches against the England squad of the late 1950s. The rest periods during swimming galas would be full of stories of how he represented the Bradfield Boys' Club from South London. Don't misunderstand him. Dad was always supportive, always proud of everything I achieved. It was just that there was no room for me to be proud of myself.

So while I cruised and underperformed in academia, the one area in which opportunity allowed me to outperform Dad easily, it mattered nothing to me. In every other area, including DIY and especially sport, I made huge efforts, replacing talent with sweat. The result was that others saw me as an achiever. When I occasionally moaned that I was not up to scratch, my friends laughed it off as false modesty, an attempt to draw attention to myself. While others might applaud you for making it to the moon, it still feels like failure when you know you are aiming for the stars.

Somehow, in my new Lake District team, I was liberated from this pressure. For a start, nobody there had even heard of my dad. The impossible hurdle did not have to be cleared; it just was not there, casting a shadow over my own efforts. I still tested myself against the others, of course, but in isolation from the need to return home to pin up the results.

There was another factor that reduced my need to compete openly. In this team, I had my own place. When it came to performing in a kayak, I was out there on my own. I'd done enough orienteering and camping and climbing to ensure that I would not be disgraced, but when the time came to head out on to the lake, already qualified as a British Canoe Union Instructor, it was like welcoming everyone else into my element. Greta certainly had the rock, others might have air, and I had water. In fact, within the mix of our team, there was a certain complementarity about our skills, which perhaps helped to bind us together in a spirit of cooperation rather than competition. The moment we saw Greta flowing up a rockface, we knew that we'd all be better off getting tips from her than trying to beat her. Likewise, when we jumped into kayaks, it was pretty clear to everyone that this was always going to be my game.

I said that the element of air belonged to another. In this case, it was the air of confidence, and that was Ollie's province. Greta may have been the beauty with shoulder-length blond hair who appeared to defy gravity, but socially Ollie rose above her and the rest of us. I might have been the canoeist, but Ollie gave the impression that she could stroll across the lake. In contrast to my own arrogance, it was not that she was showy; it was not even that she particularly pushed herself forward. It was just that she did not seem to be especially concerned with having any sort of image. She laughed easily at herself, she had a go at things even when she knew she might fall flat on her back, and underneath it all was a baseline level of competence and common sense.

Whatever the public personas of our group, and whether or not they were hiding any private neurosis, the mix worked. For three days, we just enjoyed living and playing together. By the second morning, I had completely forgotten that this was a selection process in which I should have been showing certain facets and hiding blemishes. We were just having fun, even more so than the other teams, and I felt lucky to have been placed with my new friends. It was an environment in which we were all shining. I won't say it was a place where I felt totally free to be myself, because I was still not quite sure who 'I' was, but I was at least able to discard some demons temporarily.

As we progressed through the assessments and training sessions, many of us had been keeping an eye on the item planned for the Wednesday evening. Until that point, we had been fully occupied from breakfast to lights out, with hardly a break. In recognition of the pace we were keeping up, the plan was that, after dinner, there would be a brief discussion scheduled to finish at 8.30. The centre had arranged for us to have the rest of the evening off and for a minibus to shuttle us the mile to the nearest village pub. I think quite a few of us were really looking forward to letting our hair down, so as Jim, the Personnel Manager, introduced the topic for conversation, there was an atmosphere of impatient expectation among the 40 or so assembled candidates.

'You all know that this is the YMCA. For you to be able to work here, it is certainly not a requirement that you be a Christian. However, we have many Christian groups visiting us and it is reasonably common for visitors to ask instructors questions about the Christian faith. Instructors are not required to promote Christianity but it is important that you have thought about your own views. This evening's task is to discuss in your small groups the following question: "How relevant is Jesus Christ to me?" When you feel you have discussed this thoroughly, you are free to finish. You don't need to report back, and when you are done you can take the rest of the evening off.'

Jim smiled at the muted cheer and the babble of conversation in a manner that suggested he was enjoying some private thought rather than our collective reaction. Later I came to know Jim as an extremely thoughtful, insightful man, and I have often wondered if he had anticipated some of the events that would follow before sunrise on Thursday.

As Jim left the room, the chorus of low conversation mixed with the sound of chairs being dragged across the floor into several rough circles. This evening, for the first time, our groups had been shuffled, so that, of the faces I was looking at, only Ollie's was familiar to me. Far from being disconcerted by this new cocktail, I had as my primary consideration the imminent departure of the minibus, shortly to be followed by a pint of almost anything. A quick glance at my watch informed me that we had about half an hour if we were to catch the first bus. I decided to seize control of the proceedings, in what turned out to be an ill-judged opening gambit.

'This shouldn't take long. He died two thousand years ago. I can't see how he has any significant impact on any of us. So, if we all agree to that, we can get off and I'll get the first round in.' I felt that I had delivered a preemptive strike on anyone interested in getting into the sociological and anthropological aspects of living in a society shaped by the influence of organized Christian religion. I looked around the group, expecting full agreement with my *coup de grace*. Probably, if it had not been for Ollie, that is exactly what I would have got.

'Well, I don't agree. I believe Jesus is alive today, and he is relevant to everything I do.' She was slightly flushed and the firmness of her glance told me that she was up for a fight. Even in that moment, I could not help but notice the way she managed to say 'Jesus' in the way others would say 'Mike' or 'Helen', as if she was talking about someone who joined us for lunch on most days. There was no mock childish emphasis on the first syllable, as in 'the baby *Jee*sus', which seems to be the only way most adults can bring themselves to pronounce it. In contrast, her pronunciation communicated familiarity. I turned to the rest of the group, rolling my eyes up towards the ceiling in an expression I had not used for at least four days, as if to say, 'There's always one, eh, lads?' Instead of the anticipated smirks of sarcastic agreement, a tall guy called Steve followed suit.

'I agree with Ollie. I'm a Christian, too.' He didn't deliver it with quite the same conviction, so I still reckoned on being in with a fighting chance of a swift conclusion. The supportive nods and smiles of the other three group members quickly corrected that misapprehension. Unbelievably, of the six of us, I was the only one not describing himself as a 'born-again Christian'. How unlucky could you get? Having nailed my colours so firmly to the mast at the outset, I had no option but to try to fight my way out of a corner. Attack is the best form of defence.

'How is it possible to believe in something you cannot see, hear or discuss?'

'Surely it was man who created God as a way of understanding his universe—as a crutch.'

'What about evolution? Surely you don't believe the world was created in only six days.'

'What about all the disasters? If God is so loving, how can he allow the various famines and earthquakes? How could he allow the Holocaust to happen to his own people?'

I gave it the full salvo—rehearsed all the arguments, especially the unanswerable ones, even the ridiculous ones: 'Do you seriously expect me to believe that a donkey saw an angel or talked?' I'd done a fair bit of Sunday school and I knew enough to be able to argue a bit. For the most part, the others tried to counter what I was saying, supporting each other and nodding encouragement.

We talked on... and on. I watched the time for the departure of the minibus come and go. Mind you, I found I was so enjoying the argument that missing the bus seemed little more than a minor inconvenience, and, over time, one by one, my opponents excused themselves and headed for bed. If I could call them opponents, that is. I was especially struck by their refusal to go on to the attack themselves, no matter how provocative I became. If anything, they seemed supportive of my questioning, often agreeing with me about the difficulty in reconciling the Bible with the experience of many people living on this planet. Collectively they conveyed an attitude of concern for me, as if they were helping me work through a problem rather than trying to convince me that I was wrong.

Many of the arguments I had heard before. I had attended an evangelical church between the ages of three and 14, on a pretty regular basis. It all started when my parents left their rented flat in South London for a mortgaged semi in Berkshire. When they moved, I was only a couple of months old. Dad was still working in London, commuting every day and even working weekends to afford the monthly repayments. By the time I was three, Mum, along with a neighbour, had decided it was time to start going to church with me. Her family had traditionally attended the Medical Mission in Bermondsey every Sunday afternoon, and she had even been 'churched' after I was born. 'Churching' was the practice of attending either a church or hospital chapel as soon as possible after a safe delivery, to thank God for the arrival of the baby and for the health of all involved. This ritual was taken seriously in my mother's family, with no other excursions permitted until the proper rites had been observed.

In Berkshire, away from the place where she had been brought up, away from family members and friends, Mum began to feel quite isolated, especially with Dad working so hard. In such a frame of mind, it is not surprising that she decided to find some familiar rhythms, and I guess she saw Sunday visits to church as both the 'proper' thing to do and an opportunity to meet some friends. She tried the Anglican church first, but was told that there was a waiting list for children wishing to join the Sunday school. Walking home from this rejection, she passed the doors of a small evangelical fellowship and struck up a conversation with someone on the pavement outside. She was warmly welcomed and I was allowed immediate access. Thus, with fairly few interruptions, I attended this church every Sunday morning for the next eleven or twelve years. Mum, and often Dad, came to the one family service each month. I represented the church in swimming galas, attended the occasional summer camp, and even won the county heats of a national Bible reading competition, progressing to an un-distinguished performance in the final at the Royal Albert Hall.

This all seemed, at the time, to have little lasting impact on me. There were some moments that the willing teachers there would have called highlights. On being asked what I would like for my 13th birthday, I asked for a copy of a Good News Bible, which my parents bought. I still have it. On one summer camp, I got suffici-ently swept along with the emotion of a service to talk to one of the leaders about making some form of commitment but, once back in the safety of home, I forgot all about that. As I got older, I preferred the opportunity to play rugby for a local junior side and consigned church attendance to history. All that I carried forward was a reasonable knowledge of Bible stories, the ability to recite the Old Testament books in order, ineligibility for the local grammar school and enough ammunition to combat well-meaning theological arguments.

As I was saying, the Christians excused themselves from our debate one by one. By the time it was just Ollie left, we were the only people still in the room. Everyone else had long since departed and the lights-out curfew had come and gone. We talked on. From this distance I can't remember the details of what was said but, as it came down to just the two of us, the conversation would have become more personal. I'm pretty sure she told me her testimony and I talked a little about my background. What I do recall is how impressed I was with Ollie's level of certainty. She did not seem to have all the answers and was willing to admit as much, but none of this dented her conviction. She just knew she was right in her faith. While sitting in a Student Union bar arguing over the best football team, greatest rock acts or best actors, I knew that with superior knowledge, wit or enough verve, anyone could win the debate. In this conversation it became clear that, however devastating the proof I constructed, it was not going to make any difference to Ollie. She knew she would leave the room with her faith as solid as when she had entered. I flung a fair few barbs in her direction, but her armour seemed altogether more substantial than my home-knit chain mail.

When she did eventually leave, tired but in no way bowed by the evening, I knew that my head was far too busy for sleep. More than that, there was something located closer to my stomach that was troubling, nagging, even stabbing. I glanced at my watch. It was already well past midnight, and I really should be getting some rest ahead of Thursday's activities. If it had only been my buzzing head, I might well have hit the sack, but it was the hole somewhere in my centre that was keeping me awake.

The hole wasn't new. I had known about its existence for a long time. I suppose any moderately introspective person is aware of the void at the centre of the human psyche. It is the knowledge that no experience or achievement you can generate yourself will ever be enough to leave you completely fulfilled. It allows no permanent peace but only temporary emotional highs. It can be forgotten for short periods of time. You can distract yourself, pretend it has gone, but, like a summer wasp at a pub garden bench, it buzzes round the periphery of your consciousness, demanding your attention, and you know that ignoring it will not send it away. One of my more recent tactics had been to party, to drink, but when the lights and music were replaced by more sober reflection, the hole was still there. It would swallow everything I gave it, and grow, somehow fed but never replete. Around me I saw people who, like me, were craving a hole-free existence, and others who seemed to live in ignorance of it. This latter group were deserving of a special scorn, being, in my opinion, too lacking in self-awareness even to discover what was lurking inside. I comforted myself with the knowledge that one day, most likely in the middle of some crisis, they would stumble up to the edge and peer down into their own personal abyss for the first time. To my mind, people either developed coping mechanisms or lived in blissful ignorance of the hole. It had quite simply never occurred to me that some people might be solid all the way through.

That particular night, the echoes that reverberated up from my empty tin-can depths were too loud to ignore. On such nights (and they almost always are nights), the only answer is to walk. There had been, for instance, the time when, having been dumped by one rather special girlfriend, I'd gone wandering on the Clifton Downs in Bristol, idly considering leaping from the Clifton suspension bridge as a way to silence the inner doubts. It was more the stories I'd heard of failed attempts than a fear of death that ultimately proved decisive on that occasion. The idea that I might end up alive but chest-deep in the ooze through which the ebb-tide Avon dribbled was frankly too likely and too embarrassing.

This time, however, after our debate, I aimlessly wandered the cold gravel paths that eased through the woodland to the south of the main centre buildings, hands thrust deep into pockets and head down. With only the vaguest knowledge of the direction in which I was heading, I eventually sighted hints of the lake ahead between the mossy trunks, and deliberately moved towards the shore.

Costell's Rocks are marked only on the more detailed maps of Windermere. They comprise an unremarkable collection of jagged dark lumps that can be entirely submerged when rainfall lifts the water level slightly. Usually they poke five or ten inches above the surface, just off the western shoreline and a mile or so from the southernmost tip of England's longest lake. They have been awarded a rusty red metal warning triangle and, more recently, a ring of large orange buoys to warn powerboat users of the risk of grounding. Only at exceptionally high water levels is the largest of the rocks completely surrounded by water, normally being attached to the land just where the path I was following passed closest to the gravel beach. I left the path and jumped up on to that rock. The stretch of water, my element, opened up in front of me. There was a sense of openness, of space. Immediately I felt less constrained, less weighed down. Cold though it was, I sat down to think. It was *the* moment—time to try out this Christianity business properly.

I'd love to be able to tell you that I had a sense of the convergence of key and decisive influences funnelling down to a single point in time. As the Prayer Book says, life-changing events like marriage are not to be entered into lightly or with lack of reverence, and yet it was not the consequences of my decision that I was considering with any gravity. Indeed, it seemed to me that while a commitment to God had to be genuine, it could also be taken quite lightly. It was a win–win situation. If I decided, here and now, to follow Christ, there was a chance that absolutely nothing would happen. I would stand up and go to bed, knowing that Ollie and her mates were deluding themselves and that they too would one day stumble across their own inner abyss and watch their faith sink into the depths. Either that or they would eventually die in blissful and blessed ignorance. If they were right, then I would make a transition that would eliminate my own inner emptiness once and for all, a state that until recently had seemed unattainable. All I needed to do was to take a jump of faith. There was no one to watch and, if all that followed was an embarrassed silence, then no one need ever know. It was just a question of taking that step into the unknown, to see if the invisible would actually hold my weight.

As it turned out, the final nudge I needed was not noble or logical but that very base emotion, envy. When all was said and done, I envied the apparent confidence of the Christians I had encountered this week. They just looked as if they had everything worked out and, if I followed through on the experiment, the results would allow me either to join them or to enjoy exploding their false hypothesis.

It had not been the months of Sundays at church that had ultimately convinced me to take the plunge, but they had at least provided me with a working knowledge of the mechanism. I sat, barely aware of the cold seeping through the seat of my trousers, and prayed. I admitted that I was a sinner—an easy enough step for anyone, really, considering that it simply meant admitting I had done a few things wrong, and that was not going to be news to anyone. The next step was to agree that Jesus is the Son of God, and that his death and resurrection were intended to deal with my wrongdoing, even though his actions predated them by some 2000 years. Did I honestly believe that? I think an accurate description of my attitude at that point was that I was prepared to go along with the story, if that was what it took. I pretty much glossed over this and headed straight to the third step of handing my life over to the control of God. This was much easier, given that it was the crux of my 'no lose' scenario. If he was truly a benign and all-powerful God who would sweep away my inner doubts, he was unlikely to do a worse job of running my life than I was doing. If he was none of those things, then I was back to square one, fully confirmed in my cynical stance and with no route to salvation except through pure, unadulterated hedonism.

I finished my prayer and opened my eyes.

Nothing.

Absolutely nothing happened.

I'm not quite sure what I expected. A shooting star would have been enough, but there was no celestial choir. I felt nothing—nothing, that is, except a lingering doubt that perhaps I had not shown enough willingness, enough commitment. This was an unexpected result, a different outcome from the two I had predicted seconds before. I had neither new faith nor new insight, but instead a new doubt. What if I had come right to the point of crossing over to a new experience and had fallen short at the final hurdle by not genuinely throwing myself forward? There was absolutely no way I was going to leave the rock with an added burden of uncertainty.

I lifted my head, pushed out my chin and repeated the words of my prayer, this time out loud into the still night air.

Still nothing. And still the doubt remained. Was my prayer just not enough for God? With the question came the first stirrings of anger, perhaps at the suspicion that my attempts had again not been sufficient. Not only had I failed to measure up to my earthly father, but now the heavenly one was not impressed with my efforts, either. It would have to be all or nothing.

I scrambled quickly to my feet and walked right to the edge of the rock, the toes of my boots almost touching the water. A quick glance back ensured there were no witnesses, an acknowledgment of the slight embarrassment which, although present, was not enough to divert me now. I took a full breath, steaming in the dry air. Then I shouted my prayer, full volume—head tilted back, eyes staring, screaming the words into the night.

I stopped, breathing heavily. As I finished, a very slight echo of my final syllable, the 'men' of 'Amen', drifted back to me from the wooded slopes of Gummer's Howe, beyond the east shore.

Then stillness.

Nothing.

Absolutely nothing at all. And I knew for certain that it was all a lie. The God of my Sunday school, the Father that Ollie and the others had described, would never have ignored the very best I had. He would not be cruel enough to watch my performance and hold back, deny me my promised reward. His offer was written down in the Bible in such a way that my acceptance should immediately merit consideration. The only other option left to me was that of the unbeliever, so it was as a confirmed atheist that I climbed down off the rock and walked back to my quarters, slipping quietly into my sheet sleeping bag without disturbing my room mates. I was not especially disappointed or upset. I don't recall feeling anything at all except a need to get at least some sleep before the morning. After all, it was not as if my experiment had failed; I had my answer.

When I woke, the entire world had changed.

It is not easy to describe how, but it is a sensation that many Christians will recognize. From the second my eyes opened, I knew it had happened, and I don't mean 'suspected' or 'felt' or 'had the impression'—I knew. The world was a better place than I ever remembered. The sun was brighter, the air was fresher and I was happy. Yes, that was it, I was just happy. It was not the momentary satisfaction that comes with achievement, not the laughter of some comedy moment, not enjoyment of something fun or exciting or interesting. All of these feelings are temporal, linked to a set of events, experiences that are tainted slightly by the foreknowledge that they will eventually be replaced by other, less wholesome moments. I was somehow permanently happy. It was my first experience of joy. Somehow my feet did not touch the ground and it seemed that nothing or nobody could change that.

For the best part of the day, I was content just to enjoy this new feeling. I chatted my way through breakfast and floated my way through assembling my kit and loading a trailer. I joined a small group of other experienced canoeists on a day trip down the series of minor rapids linking the tip of Coniston Water to the tidal estuary that forms the southern boundary of Cumbria. Even being physically tired at the end of the trip and chilled as we loaded the kayaks for the drive back to the centre, the day still felt like perfection. I remember singing 'Wonderful world' in a mock Louis Armstrong voice as I helped Dean, one of the centre staff, with his boat. When he raised an eyebrow at me, perhaps I just imagined in his face an understanding of the source of my high spirits—or perhaps not. I later discovered that he was already a Christian.

It was only towards nightfall that I again bumped into Ollie, and I could tell that she was desperate to ask what had happened. As it turned out, she didn't need to. She could tell just by looking at me. As we spoke, I was reminded for the first time that day of the inner void that could never be filled. In remembering, I looked inside, searching for the darkness at my centre and, in that moment, realized it had gone. I was new, remade, complete.

As I write this, looking back from a distance of 20 years, I am still not sure exactly what it was that prompted the screamed commitment across Windermere. In retelling the tale, it seems that rather than the positive experiences of childhood Bible stories and Sunday school and newfound friends, it was the negativity, the doubts, the anger and the insecurities that were crucial. I find it hard to see how, without them, I would ever have crossed over. What appeared to be the weapons of evil were, in fact, the ploughshares preparing a ground more fertile than anyone would have suspected. I recently worked as a missionary in Nepal, managing a leprosy hospital. I vividly recall speaking to Chandra, our hospital chaplain, a Nepali man whose absence of fingers and feet, collapsed nose and toothless gums speak of the ravages of leprosy. It was leprosy that had brought him to the hospital some 30 years previously, and it was there that he became a Christian. He told me that every day of his life he gives thanks for leprosy, because without it he would never have even heard the name of Jesus. While my experiences in no way compare to Chandra's, I think I know what he means.

How low can you go?

The more things a man is ashamed of, the more respectable he is.
George Bernard Shaw, 'Man and Superman' (1903)

What is the opposite of love? If you ask a schoolchild—actually, if you ask anyone in the street—I expect that once you discount the flippant, smart-alec answers you are bound to get every now and then, 100 per cent of the sensible respondents will say 'hate'. It is what they appropriately call a 'no-brainer'. It's also completely wrong. Take a little time, ignore the conditioned responses and actually apply your brain to the question. Think about it.

The answer is not 'hate'; the true answer is 'indifference'. Hate and love have a lot in common: they are both powerful emotions that increase the pulse rate, fire the adrenal glands, dilate the pupils and dilute reason. It is self-evident that to love something or someone, you have to care, to give respect. To hate, even more so. It is not worth getting all pumped up about something unless you have an interest, unless you respect it enough to recognize that it has meaning and impact in your life.

When I was a young man, if I had seen you in a pub but you had avoided eye contact and continued to chat in the corner with your friend, I would not have spared you a second thought. You would have joined the very long list of people that were beneath my consideration. Only if I had calculated that you were significant enough to be some sort of threat would I have paid you any attention, and that would probably have resulted in a fight. I was big and, by my early 20s, had seen more than enough of life in bars from London to Glasgow and everywhere in between to be able to handle myself. I was, in fact, an idiot. I had an illness, a disease that had rendered me indifferent to anyone and anything that

I encountered, with the single exception of my reflection in the mirror. I saved all my respect, all my love—and, if I think it through, most of my hate—for me. From the age of 13, I had been suffering from the debilitating, growth-stunting condition that I call rampant selfishness. All that anyone else got was the flipside, the external symptoms—arrogance, more accurately described as indifference, sneering indifference.

Of course everyone is selfish; that is part of the human condition. It develops into an illness when it becomes rampant and over-whelms all your defences. At school it really began to take hold of me, partly because I was so unprepared for the attitudes I en-countered there. I'd not developed the immunity that most other pupils had taken in with their mothers' milk. Instead I had arrived as a fertile breeding ground for infection. Without the necessary antibodies and inoculations, the disease entered my system un-checked, growing and multiplying. It took perhaps five or six years to grip me, to swamp the decent, hard-working white blood cells I had inherited.

What generated the onset of the disease for me was privilege. My DNA seemed programmed to withstand hardship, hard work, hard times, but you don't develop a resistance to infections that you and your family have never previously encountered. I was from a working-class family in north-west England. My dad's dad lied about his age to enlist for active duty in the grinding, grim slog of the First World War. When he emerged from the trenches, mud-smeared and blood-smeared, he was rushed to the infirmary. He had lost one eye, one arm, two legs from the knees down, and all of his youth. Once the hospitals had run out of ideas, he was discharged to his home in Congleton, where he had a smallholding from which he (literally) single-handedly dragged a smaller income. He married Ida who, in 1937, delivered him a son, my father, and promptly died.

My mum's dad, by comparison—but only by comparison—had it easy. When he left school at the age of 14, he headed for work as an office boy, no doubt with knitted tank top, collar button fastened, shirt neatly tucked in, probably holding his head high in an attempt to keep others from glancing at his feet. His parents could not afford to buy him shoes and so, as he was very, very fond of telling me and my siblings, his dad cut the heels off his sister's shoes for him to wear. They were not so much working class as 'scraping by' class.

My dad, the only son of a widowed, struggling smallholder, was bright—very bright. It would be impossible to know for sure, but I suspect he piled genuine application on top of his natural talent. In adult life he was a man who really worked—a solid man prepared to put in the long steady hours quietly, valuing dedication and persistence and graft, probably above those unearned, God-given talents of intellect or creativity. It seems likely to me that he took his intelligence and allied it with continuous enduring effort to achieve a scholarship to the Kings School in Macclesfield, north-west seat of learning for the privileged. You've got to respect that, haven't you?

Truth be told, I didn't. I inherited many things from my parents —enough intelligence to win a part-scholarship to an expensive public school in Shropshire, and a capacity for graft and hard work, choosing to apply it to the pursuit of instant cash over and above academic achievement. I would head down to the nearby station and offer to clean the platforms for the guards, relieving them of a job they hated along with a handful of coins. However, I was determined that the characteristics I shared with Mum and Dad would not turn me into a replica of them. In my eyes, they just did not bear comparison to the people they resented and rejected— their neighbours. Having worked to climb into the middle-class professions, they had emerged from the fog and fumes of the working class to arrive, blinking, in the light that surrounded those with money. But once their eyes had adjusted to the glare, they found that they did not like many of those who were indigenous to that altitude.

Dad had become a GP, living in a rural and generally affluent community in Shropshire. He was good at his job and proud of it. Through ability and effort he had become a professional, and through more effort he sustained his practice and a good income. He typically worked a 24-hour shift every third day, ensuring adequate cover all through the night for his patients. He provided well for us all, earning enough to pay the portion of fees that was not covered by the part-scholarship for me and the three siblings who followed me. I'm afraid the money did not stretch far enough for the youngest two, who had to make do with state-funded education. It was clearly a financial burden for our family that, ironically, left us too few resources to match the lifestyles of those among whom we lived and studied. Had we all gone to state schools, we might have had a little left over for the finer things of life.

Despite our relatively modest disposable income, it was the fact that our money had been *earnt* that was especially important to Dad. He was scornful, perhaps resentful, of those who achieved wealth without having achieved anything else. They were not 'real' people and they did not have the same understanding of the value of money that poverty had seared into my parents. Those among whom we lived were comparatively profligate with their cash, and to Dad's way of thinking they had only really earnt disdain.

I viewed the difference from another perspective. What Mum and Dad called solid and dependable, I called boring. What they regarded as ostentatious or flashy, I saw as interesting and fun. I noticed that when we returned home, it was to a family meal prepared by Mum, while it seemed that those who lived around us were always going out to restaurants. They holidayed at expensive hotels in St Tropez. When we travelled to the south of France, complete with casserole dishes full of pre-prepared meals clinking in the back of the car, it was to stay in a rented tent.

I began to resent the differences, to notice the fiscal gap between us and the others, especially those whose families paid full fees for the same classes that I attended. Even the different vocabulary eroded any residual sense of equality or superiority that I might have retained: while we had a 'settee' in our 'lounge', the other kids had homes with 'sofas' in 'drawing rooms'. I well remember one of my contemporaries receiving £1000 per month pocket money. He would casually spend 50 quid on a jacket, wear it a couple of times and then discard it. Others may not have been quite so filthy rich but they were certainly posh, coming from families to whom boarding at a public school was traditional—a right rather than a privilege. With such familiarity comes a contempt for those who have somehow scrambled together enough to gain access for the first time, and with that contempt comes an aura of personal assurance. I frequently doubted if I fitted in, while they appeared to believe they were born to it. They sure could strut, wearing blazers, striped ties and polished shoes with a nonchalance and aplomb that gave no hint of weakness.

I probably learnt more from my school peers than I cared to admit. Dislocated souls can go in almost any direction and I carried my family's reverse snobbery, my dad's appetite for work, into school long enough to add an understanding of the advantages of wealth. I also learnt to adopt the school swagger. Hypocritical? Perhaps, but in my defence it was a survival mechanism as much as anything else. Bullying was rife and those who stood out were the targets. I quickly learnt to walk tall, talk posh and affect that casual arrogance. I became one of the bullies, using my quicker-than-average wit and greater-than-average bulk to pick on some un-fortunate, all in the cause of making my mates laugh and cementing my position within the crowd. I didn't support the bullies when they turned violent—on some occasions even standing up for the poor victim—but that would not stop me lashing the same kid with my tongue next time I saw him.

I left school when I got to 15 (which was the very earliest opportunity) and feigned attendance at the local technical college. I actually spent my days at McDonalds, working, earning money. If I was going to continue to strut, I was going to need to get my hands on some cash, and I was more than happy to get my hands greasy and earn my five stars in return for beer money. I was already a regular at the local, having first been served in the village pubs at the age of 13. I'd had to fund the early drinking through theft from my parents, snatched from purses and wallets, but suddenly I had £56.85 a week to play with. When that did not quite stretch far enough, I knew which drawer held Mum's housekeeping.

I loved it. The next year, having turned 16, I left home and moved into a bedsit, mainly because then I had absolutely no distractions from the work–party–sleep–work cycle that I was revelling in. I had the bed, frequently shared with my girlfriend, while my mate Ian had the floor, often shared with his. I was sharp and bright enough to be promoted rapidly within the McDonalds operation, giving me enough money and enough time to spend it.

Sometimes a single moment can be powerfully symbolic and represent a whole era. I remember, one particular summer morning. I was on the way home from a party with Ian. The sun was just about up, the deep blue of the sky gradually paling, the clear air carrying the crisp smell of dewy grass. My head had the light, fuzzy quality that comes from being pleasantly drunk—not absolutely blasted but gently softened around the edges. I should have been in raptures. In beautiful weather, with my health, strength, vitality, lack of responsibility, steady girlfriend and good mates, I should have been congratulating myself. Instead, I turned to Ian and said the words I can quote to this day: 'If I could one day earn £120 a week, *then* I'd be happy.' I genuinely, definitely, wholeheartedly believed it—as if happiness could be bought so cheaply. My life is partly a lesson in how expensive happiness can be if you are determined to buy it with money.

Of course, I had my dad's dogged drive to help me get what I wanted. Employers will suck up that particular mixture of intelligence, ambition and youth. I quickly found myself a job as a trainee shop manager for Ratners, the jewellers. I started off in Shrewsbury, but quickly transferred to Hereford, Macclesfield, Birmingham and eventually Glasgow, where at 18 I became the youngest ever shop manager in the history of the brand, with the one exception of Gerald Ratner himself. The chain was still going strong in the days before his ill-advised speech at the Institute of Directors, so the earrings now famous for costing less than an M&S prawn sandwich were then selling well, and I did my bit, urging the staff and customers onward, ever onward.

The towns, faces and accents may have been different, but my routine did not change. Each time I arrived in town, I quickly found a girlfriend and moved in with her. Then, if a promotion did not move me on in time, I would cite boredom as the reason for breaking up with her and moving out. Behind me I left a trail of variously disillusioned, disappointed or disgusted girls, to whom I was indifferent. By the time I arrived in East Kilbride, I had perfected my returned goods refund scam, which meant I was augmenting my salary with theft from my employers. Conversely, I was hard on any staff behaviour of which I or the company disapproved. The sectarian attitudes I encountered in Scotland somewhat shocked me, and I didn't shirk from sacking one shop assistant when he refused to serve a customer who had asked to look at the Masonic rings we sold. Remorse? Not me. If I needed to hurt someone to get what I wanted, then that was the way it had to be.

While in Scotland, I passed my driving test and decided I should have a company car. Retailers rarely offer such perks so I had to find another job. I was taken on by Endsleigh, the life assurance company, and began selling for them in the London area, complete with my own set of wheels. Moving down to the hustle and drive of London marked a step-change for me. Until then, my selfishness— my disease—had allowed me to trample on a few feelings and steal from a big company. Once I had moved on to London, I found within myself the capacity to go well beyond those limits into areas of selfishness that few would contemplate. I had it bad, and because I could talk my way out of most problems and run away from anything else, I was able to live pretty fast and very loose.

I would find a flat that I liked—nicely furnished, all the mod cons—and then try a con of my own. I would move in, having paid the deposit and the first month's rent, but that was the last the landlord would get from me. It would start with a few excuses: my salary cheque was late; I'd lost my cheque book and the bank hadn't sent me another one; I just needed a few days. I could come up with any lie to fit any occasion. Then, when the excuses started wearing thin, I would just ignore the demands, pretending not to be in when the knock on the door came. I could stretch it out to about six months before I had to move on and find somewhere else to stay. In some cases, I even sold the furniture from one flat to raise the money for the deposit on the next one. Sorry, no forwarding address, and I was gone.

While I could not find money for rent, I could always find enough for booze, drinking pretty much every day and pretty heavily. Sometimes I would find a girlfriend and move in with her, which meant I did not even have to find deposit money. When one relationship became inconvenient, I would deliberately end it and find another. Once, I carelessly got a girlfriend pregnant. In my disposable world I simply borrowed £135, handed the cash over to the clinic, and the problem was gone. She was devastated, utterly floored by the emotional impact of the abortion. That was my signal to leave. I didn't need the hassle and I did not suffer any remorse, so I was unable to offer any genuine empathy.

Next I got into the business of selling photocopiers on 'cost-per-copy' contracts. The deals were shocking, a real rip-off and we knew it, but we didn't care. All we had to do was get into an office, get the deal signed and get out. Before the client knew what was happening, they had a new photocopier that was running up bills faster than they could fill the paper tray. There were a bunch of us, mostly young lads, sleeves rolled up and cigarettes burning in the ashtrays, on the phones, talking fast, cajoling the punters to let us in the door. I got a smattering of sales training—all the usual stuff about getting to 'yes'.

In the office, the boss would use peer pressure to keep us at it. If someone didn't meet the weekly targets, he put the word round and we would all give them a bit of a kicking on a Friday night. Sometimes we didn't wait for the end of the week and some poor underperformer would see a group of us surging towards him, washing over and around his desk, to give him a bit of a slap. At times we would march—literally march in step—round the block together; we would sing company songs, and always we would drink together. In some ways we were like football fans with suits, bouncing off each other, noise multiplying, feeding off the machismo and the bravado, swelling to invade the personal space of everyone unfortunate enough to be around us. On one company night out at the coast, we threw a bouncer off the Margate pier. We were no respecters of authority, decorum, anything or anyone.

Quite naturally, in a time when enterprise was everything, I then joined up with a few mates and started my own business. I was a 21-year-old entrepreneur, selling office telephone systems, but this time disaster struck. They tell you that most new businesses end in failure; mine rather crashed, and I can't honestly blame anyone other than myself. The people who listened to my patter and signed up did so because I could spin a good tale and be convincing, but as soon as I got the sale and received the money, I spent it—and I don't mean investment. On one occasion, I was paid twice by the same company because of some simple administrative error. I knew it was a mistake but by the time they discovered the slip I had spent the money twice, assuming I would get away with that too. I was summoned to court.

The way the system works is that you get put on notice that your case will come up for trial some time over the following week or so. I'd been on notice before, warranted to appear, but had never actually been called. Even so, it was always a dreadful week, waiting and wondering if the call would come. This time it did, and I was instructed to appear at Southwark Crown Court at 12.30pm the next day. I never intended to go, and the next morning I phoned the court office to explain that I would not be turning up because I was sick. I was put through to the policeman responsible for my case, and by the sound of it he was more than used to dealing with people like me.

'What's the problem? Why aren't you here?'

'I'm sick, not well.'

'Are you actually in hospital?'

'No.'

'Can you walk?'

'Yes.'

'Then you'd better be here.' I can't actually remember if he used 'sonny' as an epithet, but he may as well have done. The threat was clear: if I didn't get there on time, I would be in contempt and would not be expected to pass 'Go' on the way to jail.

I didn't get the chance to explain that I was in Stevenage and that I had, in effect, 45 minutes to get to Southwark. I slammed the phone down, ran to the car and drove in panic as hard as I could. On the dual carriageway I screamed along, squeezing between cars, forcing my way past. I figured that I may as well risk hospital, as that seemed to be the only way I would escape prison. It did occur to me that perhaps the only other excuse the judge might accept was if I got arrested for dangerous driving and was in custody elsewhere when my case was called. Somehow I made it, abandoning the car somewhere near a curb and literally running into the court.

'I'm here, I'm here,' I gasped at the clerk as the minute hand travelled towards the bottom of the clock. I only got a puzzled look; it seemed that there were two court buildings in Southwark and I was in the wrong one. Sweating, fretting, I raced through the streets—late, but fortunately not too late. Eventually, with the paperwork done, I was in the dock. That view down the steps to the dark corridor heading for the court's cells, only one step away from a line that had very few stops on the way to Brixton Prison, had the effect of bringing the consequences of my actions into sharp focus. This could be it—a disaster that I couldn't talk my way out of.

Something, though, was on my side. The judge scheduled to hear my case had a reputation for severity but was, for some reason, replaced by one more inclined to leniency. Perhaps my panicked sprint into town added the appearance of sincerity to my display of regret when I was inevitably pronounced guilty. I was ordered to settle the debt and given a six-month jail sentence but, crucially, it was suspended for two years. On the way in, I'd leapt up those three or four steps at the front of the square, grey, concrete court buildings full of dread. Much to my relief, I was able to descend those same steps, albeit more slowly, still a free man—just.

This was a new chance, a new life, a fresh opportunity to get my life on track and sort things out. I'd been spared the downward spiral of prison followed by unemployment, followed by more crime, followed by longer stays at Her Majesty's pleasure.

It was perhaps a measure of my utter stupidity that I completely ignored the lifeline. I went straight back to the same pubs, the same life, the same mates. And that debt? Oh, yeah, that. I didn't give it a second thought and I certainly didn't pay it. I didn't use the guilty verdict or the jail term suspended above me as a spur to turn things around. There was still further for me to fall first—much further.

Inevitably, within a year, my business collapsed. I got a phone call from one of my partners. 'It's all gone wrong. We've gone bust. There's heavies at the office. Don't go back there. I've legged it.'

For some reason, I didn't run. Instead I headed back to the office to see what was going on. When I walked into the reception area, there were two blokes waiting for me, clearly not there to buy telephone systems. As they stepped forward to meet me, I shook their hands and introduced myself, acting on some sort of salesman autopilot. The two of them—one small with his hair pulled back tightly in a ponytail, the other huge and bearded—accepted my invitation to come to the main office. As they got in the lift with me, the big guy opened his jacket to show me the gun he was carrying.

When the lift doors opened at our main office, it was on to a scene of chaos, with a bunch of thugs making it pretty clear to the frightened employees that they wanted some answers, including the whereabouts of the management. There were papers scattered across desks, phones left unanswered, dogs, knives and the smell of fear. It became clear that my partner had hired some people with some very, very bad relatives. Not only that, but he had borrowed money from them and, as a form of security, had given these people his home address. When the repayments did not arrive, the debt collectors tried to pay him a visit, only to find that the address he had given was actually that of a fruit and veg shop in Chigwell. They were the sort of people who express their disappointment very vividly, so, knowing this and pausing only to give me a call, my partner had just disappeared.

I think what saved me from serious injury was that instead of simply quivering outwardly, I attempted to discuss solutions in a reasonable way. Perhaps my life was so chaotic that I had ceased to care very much even about myself and, with very little to lose, most threats become irrelevant. I started to pay back the debt with any cash I could raise. With my business gone and no other assets, I quickly lost what little I had left. Without a car and without the means to pay rent, I lost my flat and had to sleep rough.

To those who have never had to sink to this level, it is hard to express just how awful a night on the street can be. Huddled in a doorway, desperately trying to cling on to any remaining warmth but feeling it slip out into the concrete step and brick walls, the sleepless hours stretch on interminably. I quickly worked out that Euston Station, when closed, was the best place to get some shelter from that bitter enemy of the homeless, the rain. The only way to avoid being cleared out of the station by the police was to look like a genuine traveller. To do that, I needed a valid ticket for a morning train, and the cheapest of those cost £5.60 to Hemel Hempstead. On some days, my only objective was to end up with enough money to buy the ticket and, with that prize, to look decent and normal enough to escape eviction from the concourse. On other days, without even the price of a train ticket, all I had left was my pride, and that was sufficient to prevent me from calling my parents. Surely this was as low as it could get. Surely I would bounce back.

One of my casual girlfriends was Katie, a married woman. I managed to borrow a little money from her, enough to pay a week up front for a frayed and filthy hotel room in north London. I told the manager that I was working for a company that had sent me to the city for six months, and a cheque to cover the rent would be arriving any day. It was clearly only a temporary respite. My dodgy creditors were more effective than the police in tracking me down and were still chasing me for money, while the hotel was clearly running out of patience with me and my non-existent company. I could see that I was not far from a return to the streets. I was desperate and getting more desperate. I was tired of running and fighting and struggling. I wanted to lie down, to sleep and know that I would not have to wake up to fight again.

Stealing £600 from Katie, I bought sleeping pills—a lot of them — from a pharmacy. Then I went to an off-licence and bought a litre of whisky. Appropriately equipped, I went back to the hotel room and wrote my suicide notes. I wrote them in a measured way, considering the words carefully and going through a few drafts to make sure I got them exactly right. After all, I wasn't going to be around to correct any misinterpretation. Having finished them, addressed them to Mum and Dad and to my lover who had unwittingly funded my departure, I had to set about getting in the mood. I took Katie's bank card and drew 50 quid out at a cash-point. At noon on the appointed day, I strolled into a pub somewhere in Finsbury Park. My intention was to get drunk, head back to the room, wash down all 48 pills with the whisky and fall asleep, never to wake up—and, in one last salute to the world, cheat the hangover.

By two in the afternoon, I had worked my way through four or five pints. It was a barn of a pub, a huge open room built to crowd in the fans on a Saturday afternoon before and after the Arsenal matches at the stadium nearby—the sort of place in which I could hide, even though it was far from full, with the odd social afternoon drinker and a handful of locals. Pretty quickly I'd hooked up with a couple of girls and we were chatting. That is to say, I was laughing and joking, buying drinks and giving any casual observer the impression that I had just won the lottery. I was getting on well with the girls and a small alteration to the plan was developing in my mind, which featured a little casual sex before I killed myself. I'd had enough experience talking girls into bed, playing the fool, to know that I was on to a winner. It seemed appropriate that my last act might be another selfish use of another human being, just to lighten my mood.

It was getting on towards three o'clock when I excused myself and headed for the gents. The facilities consisted of one of those functionally long troughs, designed to make the football fans feel at home and with enough space to ensure that there was not too much drinking time wasted in queueing. On a weekday afternoon, however, I had it all to myself. I've spent enough time in the wrong sort of boozer to know that, especially when you have your face to the wall, it is wise to be aware of people entering and leaving the room, and to know when someone is acting in any way out of the ordinary. I heard the door open and close and the footsteps stop behind me.

'I need to talk to you.'

The voice was not aggressive, not even very sure of itself, quivering slightly. More curious than concerned, I half turned to look over my shoulder and down at the man. He was an older man, somewhere close to 60, I'd guess, clearly uncomfortable. Just what I needed—some old gay geezer making a pass at me in a pub toilet! I turned back to look at the grubby tiled wall in front of me.

'—— off, mate. I'm not interested.' You are going to have to forgive me the language, I'm afraid.

'No, no, you don't understand,' he stammered. 'I just want to talk to you.' I had a notoriously short fuse, especially when I'd had a few, and I was going to nip this in the bud. I finished what I had come in for and turned on him, deliberately aggressive.

'—— off, mate, or I'll —— smack you.' It would be a quick fight. I was 22 years old, 16 stone, over six foot tall and drunk enough not to be inhibited about hitting an older bloke. I towered over this little man. To emphasize the difference, I was still standing up on the step in front of the trough—not that I needed any unfair advantage. I glared down at him and, as I did, I could see he was not up for a fight. If anything, he was looking embarrassed, more embarrassed than anyone I had ever seen before. He clearly did not want to be there, talking to this dangerous and unpredictable young bull, yet he carried on.

'You're in trouble.' It was not a threat but a statement of fact. As he said it, I felt as though he had punched me in the stomach. I was certain I'd never met him before. If he'd seen me in the pub, he would have thought I had nothing whatsoever to worry about, save choosing which of my two women to take back to my bed. Yet he spoke as if he knew with certainty that I had problems, as if he knew what was going on behind my eyes, behind my mouth. I tried to hide my surprise.

'What the —— are you talking about? I'm having a few drinks and I've just pulled, so why don't you just —— off?'

'No. You're in trouble.' I could see that as well as being embarrassed he was scared, really scared, and probably rightly so—but despite this, he didn't budge. He kept talking, even though he clearly would rather have been almost anywhere else. He was battling against his nerves to get the words out, stuttering. 'I was told to come in here and tell you that I know you're in trouble and that Jesus loves you and wants you to know that you mustn't give up.'

'What?' There was nothing else I could say. How could I respond to that? He had just laid me bare, reached right into my chest and squeezed all the pretence out of me. And now (or so it seemed to me) he somehow seemed to grow, as if a load was being lifted from him. He tried again, more fluent this time.

'Jesus loves you and you mustn't give up. And he told me to

come in here and tell you that.' With that, his transformation was complete. He straightened up, freed of his burden of responsibility. Having discharged his duty, with an obvious relief and perhaps a bit of pride in his own bravery, he turned and left. I'd never seen him before and I've never seen him since.

I just stood there and let him go. I could hear the clinking of glasses and shouted conversation of the real world muffled by the toilet door, and the echoing drip of water in one of the cisterns. It was a moment of stillness, a pause. Beneath my feet was the cold, hard reality of a damp concrete floor. Around me were the cracked tiles and scratched formica toilet doors, smeared with obscene graffiti— hardly an environment for a heavenly encounter, yet to this day I am not sure if it was an angel or a man that I met there.

The moment passed. I went back into the pub, got rid of the two girls, had another pint, walked back to the hotel, chucked the pills down the toilet and drank the whisky.

The next day, I did wake up to meet the hangover I deserved. I also had a new plan. It wasn't a particularly clever plan—more of a gambler's last chance than a sensible idea—but I decided to give it one more roll of the dice. A few weeks earlier, I had done a deal with a man called Phil. In sales, like any other profession, information and contacts are very valuable. I had sold Phil a stolen database of names, addresses and phone numbers. He made it pretty clear to me that if I sold or gave the list to anyone else, he would find out and he would not be happy. Of course, I had sold it several times before and several more times afterwards. It was a near certainty that Phil would know I had ripped him off. If he saw me again, he was likely to hit me, but my plan was to go and ask him for a job.

It was a stupid idea, doomed to failure. I climbed on to a tube train to get to his office and chewed over the idea. It had no basis in logic or reason, yet I had a conviction that I should give it a try. I missed my stop in my uncertainty, almost paralysed, and sat and stared into space for another entire lap of the Circle line—an hour of rattling in and out of shadow, squealing into stations and humming out of them, preoccupied with the alternate arrival and departure of determination and doubt. In the end, I struck a deal with God. I had prayed before, all those normal childish wishlist prayers. This time I agreed to give it a go, to turn up and ask for the job, but I threatened God with my own death if he didn't come up with the goods, and this time no pub angel would stop me.

Miraculously, it worked. My rung on the bottom of the ladder was a job selling photocopiers and phones, living in my red Peugeot 205 diesel company car. For four months, my home address was Toddington Services (northbound) on the M1. I'd sleep in the back of the car, get up, shower and wash my shirt in the truck drivers' facilities, stuff my duvet in the boot and go and make my sales calls. I might have been a wreck of a human being but I could still sell, and as I did the commissions started to arrive, initially as a trickle, then a steady flow. The confidence and comfort of an income was a relief after the mess and uncertainty of the previous year.

I was still seeing Katie and, in due course, she divorced her husband and we got married. For me, it was another piece in the stability jigsaw as I assembled a new set of circumstances that suited me. Why did Katie agree to it? I suppose you would have to ask her, but I was a pretty good salesman.

I was good enough to start scrabbling back up the career ladder, bad enough to plumb new depths simultaneously. Promotion, job changes, new cars, a nice house in Burton-on-Trent, foreign holidays, two children. In the next few years I accumulated them all, but mostly I accumulated money. I sucked it in, raked it towards me and, finding that it had no value when it came to filling that hole deep inside, I spewed it back out. Everything other than the earning of more cash was inconsequential. I worked a lot, and when I wasn't working I was at the bar.

Actually, a lot of the time when I was working I was at the bar, too. It meant that pretty much every night for as many as ten years, I drank several pints of lager and a bottle or two of wine. Home late, nights away, up early, battling the hangover and away to work.

Drinking with customers, drinking with colleagues, drinking with mates. It was a way to escape. I was not in love with my wife—I never had been—so heading home sober was not an especially attractive option. I was clearly not being a good father: any brief encounter with my kids at home was enough to remind me of that. However, it may be that what I was running away from was that empty feeling. Even with the streets a distant memory, bills paid and earning far more than that £120 a week, I was still unhappy.

Susan was Katie's best friend. She and I shared a drunken kiss, a bed and a six-week secretive affair, and then we moved in together. Read it quickly and perhaps you will miss the web of hurt, despair, hate and complication that we dragged along in our thoughtless, selfish wake. My two children and Susan's two children were good friends. One of the things we shattered was the simplicity and freedom of their relationships, dragging them quickly from a world of Top Trumps and Barbie clothes to muted conversations and uncertain glances, no one ever quite sure exactly where they stood. You can't replace stolen innocence, no matter how much money you earn, and I would say that my daughter has never forgiven me for the theft of hers. The four children, as so often in these cases, became tools in the mess of the four adults' broken relationships. Katie would attempt to hurt me by stopping me from seeing my kids, and I regularly lost any meaningful contact with them.

Susan and I moved to Aberystwyth. My divorce from Katie came through and the settlement just about cleaned me out. Fortunately, I also closed the biggest sales deal of my life and pulled in about a quarter of a million pounds. I was 35, and in one deal I had earnt fractionally more than £120 for every one of the 1820 weeks that I had been alive. That should be a cause for celebration, shouldn't it?

I may not have been as happy as I had once predicted, but I did know how to celebrate. On 25 June 2002, I went out for dinner and drinks with some clients in Birmingham. Of course, I got drunk. Of course, the alcohol had its usual effect, bringing out the aggressive side of my competitive nature. Of course, I had a fight. Of course, the hotel manager tried to remove me from the bar, but of course I found a way round that, paying the night staff to bring drinks out to me in the reception area. Of course, me being invincible and all that, at five in the morning I climbed into my Mercedes. It was all so predictable, so self-destructive, so inevitable.

At ten minutes past six, having had no sleep and still drunk, I fell asleep in my car, travelling at about 90 miles per hour. When it smashed into and under a white transit van, breaking the drivers' legs, the converging speed of the two vehicles was about 140 miles per hour. I was cut from the car and, with the van driver, was rushed to intensive care, where they did not expect me to live. I was in a coma for six weeks. During that period, Susan and my parents were told on seven separate occasions that they should come in and say their goodbyes because I was not expected to last the night—but, undeservedly, I lived.

As I came out of the coma, I experienced for a mercifully short time a half-world existence, in which I was aware of what was happening around me, could hear what was being said but could make no movement or sound to betray my consciousness. People would come in and talk to me, unaware that I could hear them. On one occasion, my sister-in-law was telling me about the decorating she was planning to do in her bathroom, going on and on about the colour of tiles and wallpaper. With my brain I was screaming at her to shut up, to stop boring me to tears with her trivial drivel, but it was all in my head and she just kept on talking.

Eventually it became clear that I was going to make a good recovery and I moved to the rehabilitation wards. The doctors bolted my bones back together with a collection of seven metal plates and 37 screws, but the sight in my right eye was lost for ever. The hospital recommended that I stay for a full six months, through to Christmas, but towards the beginning of September I had had enough of institutional life. I went home in a wheelchair, ignoring the medical advice and discharging myself.

My immediate arrival home was characterized not by a period of reflection or relief, but by a new fear. I was scared that this was it, the end of everything that I was about—the working, selling, joke-telling, drinking machine. If I had to sit around the house all day, I might find enough sober time to reflect on my basic unhappiness, to consider the idiot that I was. The noise of the crowd, the excitement of the deals, the calculating of percentages and the clinking of celebratory glasses drown out the sorrows, hide the truths, mask the pain. My focus became to get out of the wheelchair and get back to work.

By October, I was back behind the wheel. Actually, I had to hire a driver to hold the steering wheel because my injuries were such that I could not drive. The plus side was that this made it possible for me to keep working and keep drinking. If anything, even though I was in plaster, I lived harder, desperate to prove to myself that I was indeed indestructible—to show others that I could still sell, I could still hold court at the bar, I could come back bigger and badder than ever.

Susan took the full force, not least because now I had no reason whatsoever to ease off the booze for a drive home. My driver could deliver me there as the aggressive monster that I became when drunk. We argued, endlessly. When I had been in a coma, I'd been much easier to be with, and Susan had stayed by my bedside for up to 20 hours a day during those six weeks. During that time, she would have been hoping and even praying that I would come back. Be careful what you ask for, because I suspect she pretty soon regretted it. By Christmas of the year of my accident, having been out of hospital for about three months, we split up and I slipped straight back into the destructive cycle that had already taken me to within inches of death at least twice.

I quickly found another relationship—again with a married woman, again with two children. Again I had a fight with Katie and lost the right of access to my own children. Again I started to wreck another marriage. I was drinking so much that a great deal of that time is lost to me now, a series of incoherent memories. On one night out in Paris, I tried to fight seven men for no sensible reason (could there ever be one?) that I can recall. I was a mess.

Something in me somewhere must have known what was going on, because I started searching for some central purpose, some meaning. I bought some motivational posters, some daily reminders that might encourage me to pull myself round and in the right direction. I did some fundraising—a little selfless act so that perhaps I might not hate myself quite so much, might even feel a little virtuous. I even went to the church in my village. I had been to church before, of course. While married to Katie and living in Burton-on-Trent, I had popped into the local CofE on the occasional Sunday morning. At my expensive school I had been required to attend chapel—so many times, in fact, that I began to take pride in recognizing that I had memorized the service book better than the priest, who had to look at the words every now and then. I'd been confirmed at the age of ten, mainly because the older kids had done it and were allowed to take Communion as a result. It was the equivalent of a religious 11+, something to be gone through at a certain stage on the conveyor belt of growing up.

The village church did little to change my views. Just by walking into the building I increased the attendance by 15 per cent and lowered the average age considerably. Having yawned through the service, I walked out to my car convinced more than ever that Christianity was on its last geriatric legs. I told my driver as much.

'I should start buying and developing churches, because they are all going to be empty pretty soon.'

'Have you tried St Mike's?' he answered.

'No. Have you?' I shot the response back to him almost as an accusation, and he was quick to defend himself.

'No, no. I've just heard that it's busy.'

I went along. From the outside, down close to the sea front, St Michael's looks like any other Anglican church, with its big brown stone bell tower and arched windows. Inside, it was different. Actually, it wasn't the building that was different—it was the people.

For a start, there were loads of them; it was packed, with maybe 300 there. They were of all different ages—young families, teenagers, students, people older than me—and they all looked normal. In fact, some of them looked as though they themselves were on the dodgy side of normal, not the bunch of Thora Hirds I had been expecting. With my arrogance and cycnicism, I wanted to hate them but actually found myself envying them. There seemed to be a peace and freedom about them, an assurance, a confidence that had depth to it. When they sang the songs, they really sang them, belted them out, got lost in them. Until then, I'd been used to a half-embarrassed drone through some poorly rendered hymn, but this congregation clearly comprised people who, without any obvious hesitancy, were enjoying singing. One might say that they were worshipping.

The surprise was not enough to make me change much about my life, but it was enough to make me go again. I started to go every week, or at least every week that I was sober. I became a regular and even enrolled for an Alpha course. When I turned up for the first 'Christianity—Boring, Irrelevant, Untrue?' session in September, I found that almost everyone else on the course was a student, so I dropped out, but I kept going to the Sunday services. Swept along by the emotion and positive energy of some occasions, I would join in with the prayers asking Jesus to 'come into my life', whatever that involved. I didn't really mean it. In fact, I still didn't really know who Jesus was. I'd got to the state where the religion, the going to church, was an uplifting part of my week but I really didn't want it to impact the rest of life too much. I was still drinking, still chasing women, still living fast and loose. I even once promised the slot-machine God that I would let him come into my life as long as he let me have an Aston Martin DB7 before I died!

In January 2004, though, I had another shot at the Alpha course. This time there was much more of a mix of people involved, so I hung in long enough to discover that the Christians didn't seem to have surrendered their fun in accepting God. They had a laugh.

Not only that, but they had a laugh that didn't turn sour or involve exploiting or attacking someone, and they probably would not wake up regretting it the next morning. Their fun actually *was* funny. Yes, to my surprise, I liked them. However, I also met someone who was even more real than these people, and he was the real Jesus.

I think I'd pretty much always believed in God. I'd taken him for granted in the way we accept gravity and taxes: we might try to cheat them but there is an inevitability about them, and in the end it is better to tolerate them than buck the system. The idea that this world and the humans that rattled around in it were a cosmic fluke of molecular physics just didn't seem to hold true with me. I had no problem with the idea of God as a creator. It was the idea of Jesus that I had never really looked at properly. I guess I'd written him off as a nice bloke who said nice things and did nice things in a sickly sweet way—a bearded, white-robed wimp. But on the Alpha course I was forced to confront Jesus and start to understand what he was really like. He came out of the pages at me as a rebellious, confrontational, strong, revolutionary, wild figure. I liked him. This was someone I could relate to. He didn't compromise, didn't back down; he fought, especially for those who could not fight for themselves. He was the sort of person who would confront a big, dangerously unpredictable, drunken man in the toilets of a north London pub and tell him the hard truth, risking personal injury in the process. I'd met him before; I just didn't recognize him the first time.

As part of the Alpha course, a residential weekend away was organized, mainly to look at the Holy Spirit. During the weekend, all sorts of bizarre stuff happened that I was not quite ready for: people speaking in strange tongues and falling over. I was not comfortable with it all. It just felt a bit stage-managed, a bit forced. Angry at the nonsense that was going on, I walked out. Then I did two things that were completely uncharacteristic of me. I calmed down, and I surrendered. I just gave up.

I prayed.

'Lord, I want you in my life and I will do anything you want me to do if you'll be with me always.'

By that I even meant going back into the building and facing some of that crazy Holy Spirit stuff. I'd like to tell you that, as I completed the prayer, something seismic and remarkable happened, but nothing did.

One week later, at the beginning of March 2004, I was walking down a town street with my six-year-old son, Alex, holding his hand. My daughter, Caitie, was also with us but she was certainly not up for hand-holding. In fact, she was giving me a scowl, making it very clear that I was still not being granted privileged access to her life, having walked out on her some years before. Alex, perhaps because of his relative youth, was more forgiving. He tugged at my hand and looked up at me.

'Happy new you, Dad.'

'What, son?' I thought I had misheard. It wasn't New Year, it was early March.

'Happy new you,' he repeated. 'You're like a brand-new person.'

That was the moment when I knew something had happened, something substantial and permanent and real. Something had changed and I had become that new person, that new creation that they sang about in St Michael's. It may have taken me a week to realize it, but I had become a Christian.

In some ways, life continued as normal. I still had business problems and since then I have had a business collapse under me, and risked losing my house again. But in more important ways, life is completely different. I have been freed from my addiction to alcohol and even freed from that more pervasive addiction to money. I have a better relationship with those close to me than I have ever had before. The hard casing round my heart has cracked open, and I realize that God loves me, and being something lovable has helped to release much of the burden of self-hate that darkened my life.

In the days when I went to St Mike's but had yet to surrender totally, it was fear that held me back. I thought that if I went in fully for the Jesus 'stuff', I would have to give up so much, miss out on so many things, become somehow less of a person. What I can tell you now is that from the vantage point of this vibrant, multi-coloured experience of being a son of God, my previous existence looks like precisely what it was—a monochrome struggle, devoid of joy and populated only by false and temporary pleasures. When I lived in that greyness, I didn't even know what colour was. If you are in there, aching your way through a semi-darkness, I'd love you to come and join me in this light. If Jesus can catch the attention of someone as stupid and inward-looking as me, then I find it hard to believe that there is anyone unreachable. No matter how deep you think you are, there is a lifeline. Just grab it.

÷

Conclusion

It's the question from the BBC's *A Question of Sport* that Derek Coleman used to pose to Emlyn Hughes or Bill Beaumont or Willy Carson. These days, when Sue Barker asks the same question, the action in some sporting event is frozen and the contestants try to guess what unlikely incident follows. In the late 1990s, the TV production company that makes the programme did some market research and discovered that it was the viewers' favourite part of the show. It seems we love the suspense, but we also want to know the ending.

Of the six men in this book, three have gone on to some form of full-time Christian service: two went to work for overseas Christian organizations, while another graduated from Bible college and became the pastor of a small free evangelical church. The other three remain heavily involved in their respective churches and have continued in secular employment.

I think all of the contributors would be quick to point out that, having made a faith commitment, their lives did not immediately become one long string of answered prayers and uninterrupted blessing. One has since been married and divorced, and another has experienced business insolvency, for example. A couple of them have had further extraordinary experiences that would make good subjects for books of their own. They have all found that becoming a Christian does not make life easy: it can bring challenges, persecution and problems as well as blessing and joy. Some contributors talk of recent times of despair and loneliness, while others have seen the miraculous.

Life as a Christian, it seems, continues to be varied, exciting, sometimes awful and sometimes wonderful. So where is the difference? Well, I think everyone involved in the book would say that they are learning to view the ups and downs of life, both pre-

and post-conversion, from a different viewpoint. They can see that the great highs have often—and the deep lows always—been used in the process of their development. God may well have been involved in their lives from the very beginning, but he certainly did not stop shaping them once he had got their commitment, using many different situations in the process. However, recognizing that this is taking place and taking on trust that the ongoing journey has a beautiful end point gives it all a bit more purpose, a little more sense.

I don't like to describe the work I put into this book as research, because all I did was listen to stories and write a few of them down. Every time I heard a story, I felt privileged, challenged and excited. I also felt that each story gave me another tiny insight into the way God shapes and moulds lives, how he gets involved with us and touches us. One of my friends started his personal account by saying, 'God had always been involved in my life, in the incidents and happenings.' I think every man represented in this book, and many others, would echo that comment.

It goes without saying (but I'll say it anyway) that every story is unique. Before I started the project, though, I expected to find some patterns and some common themes. As I read the stories back, there are certainly one or two things that strike me.

The first is that in every case, just when our masculine hero needs a nudge in the right direction, there is a woman who proves to be important. It seems that God is not above using sex in his advertising and, much as we would like to think we are more complex than that, it seems that we fall for it. Perhaps men really are all the same. We seem to be designed to be dragged around by our more basic urges, and God is clearly not too high-minded or prudish to use them to get our attention.

Second, in every single story, there are people who have made a significant contribution to helping these men find God, often unwittingly. Every day, Christian men and women are meeting people, speaking to them and living with them, and among those billions of tiny actions are critical events that become important, sometimes decades later, in the shaping of lives. It seems that such is the nature of God that he often prefers not to let us see the consequences of our actions, and I wonder if that is for our protection. Would it not be a daunting responsibility to know that every little thing we do has potentially cosmic significance? On the other hand, wouldn't it be wonderful to know that the time we gave up to lead Sunday school, only to feel like an unqualified babysitter, actually did make a difference?

I'd like to think that we can respond to this fact in a couple of ways. First, be encouraged. Without knowing it, you might be as big as Billy Graham. Who knows how many people you have nudged along the path, how many times God has used something you have done to further his plans to rescue some poor individual? He is probably hiding it from you because he does not want you to get too carried away with your own importance. Regardless of that, what you do matters.

Second, you can be an encourager. If you think back over your own story and identify those people who made a difference to you, perhaps you might ask yourself how many of them you have ever thanked. I know that the majority of contributors to this book have been prompted to go back to find old friends, girlfriends, acquaintances and teachers and thank them. For some, this has taken quite some doing because they have had to confront forgiveness and reconciliation as part of the process, and I salute that. But just think about the payback. How wonderful must it feel when someone comes and thanks you for playing a part in helping them find their way to God?

Finally, there is the question of what constitutes true courage. We are brought up to honour those who show courage, to respect those who face their fears. In looking at the way in which the men in this book have made that final commitment to faith, it seems to me that the crucially courageous step is to let go, even if we are more or less ignorant of the consequences. In general, we like to be in control, to be able to calculate the risks and weigh our options.

The men in this book often used phrases like 'letting go', 'surrendering' or 'giving in' when describing that moment of ultimate commitment to God. None of them seemed to know exactly what they were going to find when they ceased to cling on—where they might 'fall' to. For them, the big step was not to put their trust in God but to stop putting their trust in themselves, to admit that they were not making such a great job of life, to relax their grip and just see what would happen. Once they did that, far from falling, they all found that God rushed up to meet them.

The courage that these men showed was to face up to their own weakness. Once they had done that, they quickly realized that to commit to God was a no-brainer. They had nothing to lose and everything to gain. It was not a deep knowledge of God or theology or even the Bible that was crucial. So consider this. Next time you are speaking to a man about faith, perhaps you should not try arguing that God is the answer. Instead, ask him if he believes that he is himself the answer, because getting past that misconception may be the biggest challenge.

As Jesus pointed out, the rest is child's play!

★ Also from BRF ★

Seeking Faith—Finding God

Getting to grips with questions of faith

John Rackley

What does it mean to be a disciple of Jesus, living according to his Gospel today? Part of the challenge of following that path is how we communicate what we believe to friends, neighbours, colleagues and family members. But how do we explain ourselves to a society that is profoundly ignorant of God's revelation?

This book shows how our witness gains authenticity when we develop a seeking and searching faith: 'If we are to communicate what we believe, it must be as fellow travellers in these difficult and demanding times.' In five sections of reflections—A yearning faith; A gospel place; Gospel encounters; Faith companions; Praying the gospel—author John Rackley wrestles with the challenge to develop such a faith and looks at what we can learn from those who first followed in Jesus' footsteps.

ISBN 978 1 84101 543 9   £6.99
Available from your local Christian bookshop or, in case of difficulty, direct from BRF using the order form on page 159.

ORDER FORM

REF	TITLE	PRICE	QTY	TOTAL
543 9	*Seeking Faith—Finding God*	£6.99		

POSTAGE AND PACKING CHARGES						
Order value	UK	Europe	Surface	Air Mail	Postage and packing:	
£7.00 & under	£1.25	£3.00	£3.50	£5.50	Donation:	
£7.01–£30.00	£2.25	£5.50	£6.50	£10.00	**Total enclosed:**	
Over £30.00	free	prices on request				

Name _____ Account Number _____

Address_____

_____ Postcode _____

Telephone Number _____ Email _____

Payment by: ☐ Cheque ☐ Mastercard ☐ Visa ☐ Postal Order ☐ Maestro

Card no. ☐☐☐☐ ☐☐☐☐ ☐☐☐☐ ☐☐☐☐

Expires ☐☐ ☐☐   Security code ☐☐☐   Issue no. ☐☐☐

Signature _____ Date _____

All orders must be accompanied by the appropriate payment.

Please send your completed order form to:
BRF, 15 The Chambers, Vineyard, Abingdon OX14 3FE
Tel. 01865 319700 / Fax. 01865 319701 Email: enquiries@brf.org.uk

☐ Please send me further information about BRF publications.

Available from your local Christian bookshop.   BRF is a Registered Charity

Resourcing your spiritual journey

through...

- Bible reading notes
- Books for Advent & Lent
- Books for Bible study and prayer
- Books to resource those working with under 11s in school, church and at home

- Quiet days and retreats
- Training for primary teachers and children's leaders
- Godly Play
- Barnabas RE Days

For more information, visit the **brf** website at **www.brf.org.uk**